FREEDOM T

C000203988

Wens
and
Swaledale

THE NORTHERN YORKSHIRE DALES

Wensleydale
and
Swaledale

THE NORTHERN
YORKSHIRE DALES

Andrew Bibby

The Ramblers

FRANCES LINCOLN

FREEDOM TO ROAM

The Freedom to Roam guides
are dedicated to the memory of
Benny Rothman

Frances Lincoln Ltd, 4 Torriano Mews, Torriano Avenue, London NW5 2RZ
www.franceslincoln.com

First published by Frances Lincoln 2006

British Library Cataloguing in Publication Data
A catalogue record for this book is available from the British Library

ISBN 0-7112-2554-0
Printed and bound in Singapore by Kyodo Printing Co.
9 8 7 6 5 4 3 2 1

Frontispiece photograph: Near Gunnerside, Swaledale

Contents

Before you go – a checklist

- *Are access-land restrictions in place?*
  Access land may be subject to temporary or permanent restrictions. Check at www.countrysideaccess.gov.uk or on 0845 100 3298.

- *Are weather conditions appropriate?*
  When poor weather is forecast, it may be sensible to postpone some of the walks in this book.

- *Do you have suitable equipment?*
  High ground can be significantly colder and more exposed than valley areas. A map and compass are recommended.

- *Does someone know where you are going?*
  If walking in a remote area, it is a good idea to leave details of your route and time of return.

- *Do you want to take a dog?*
  In general, you should assume that you will *not* be able to take dogs on open country. Most of the moors covered by this book have dog-exclusion orders in place. Check on the website or helpline given above.

- *Are birds nesting?*
  Between March and June open country is home to many ground-nesting birds. To find out where conservation restrictions are in force, check on the website or helpline given above.

Acknowledgements

The author gratefully acknowledges the assistance given him by a wide range of individuals and organizations, and is particularly grateful for the help offered by Kate Conto and Dan French of the Ramblers' Association and Kate Cave and Fiona Robertson at Frances Lincoln. Also much appreciated has been the assistance offered by staff of Yorkshire Dales National Park Authority, Mike Gill (Northern Mine Research Society), Dick Capel (East Cumbria Countryside Project), members of Yorkshire Archaeological Society, Phil Warren (Black Grouse Recovery Project), Ruth Annison (Wensleydale Railway), Colin Speakman, Andrew Hopper, Richard Peters, Paul Ticher, Maureen Wagner, Anne Hoggarth, Angie Cairns, Joanna Bibby Scullion and Jane Scullion.

Series introduction

This book, and the companion books in the series, celebrate the arrival in England and Wales of the legal right to walk in open country. The title for the series is borrowed from a phrase much used during the long campaign for this right – Freedom to Roam. For years, it was the dream of many to be able to walk at will across mountain top, moorland and heath, free of the risk of being confronted by a 'Keep Out' sign or being turned back by a gamekeeper.

The sense of frustration that the hills were, in many cases, out of bounds to ordinary people was captured in the song 'The Manchester Rambler' written by one of the best-known figures in Britain's post-war folk revival, Ewan MacColl. The song, which was inspired by the 1932 'mass trespass' on Kinder Scout when walkers from Sheffield and Manchester took to the forbidden Peak District hills, tells the tale of an encounter between a walker, trespassing on open land, and an irate gamekeeper:

He called me a louse, and said 'Think of the grouse',
Well I thought but I still couldn't see
Why old Kinder Scout, and the moors round about,
Couldn't take both the poor grouse and me.

The desire, as Ewan MacColl expressed it, was a simple one:

So I'll walk where I will, over mountain and hill
And I'll lie where the bracken is deep,
I belong to the mountains, the clear running fountains
Where the grey rocks rise ragged and steep.

Some who loved the outdoors and campaigned around the time of the Kinder Scout trespass in the 1930s must have thought that the legal right to walk in open country would be won after the Second World War, at the time when the national parks were being created and the rights-of-way network drawn up. It was not to be. It was another half century before, finally, Parliament passed the Countryside and Rights of Way Act 2000, and the people of England and Wales gained the legal right to take to the hills and the moors. (Scotland has its own traditions and its own legislation.)

We have dedicated this series to the memory of Benny Rothman, one of the leaders of the 1932 Kinder Scout mass trespass who was imprisoned for his part in what was deemed a 'riotous assembly'. Later in his life, Benny Rothman was a familiar figure at rallies called by the Ramblers' Association as once again the issue of access rights came to the fore. But we should pay tribute to all who have campaigned for this goal. Securing greater access to the countryside was one of the principles on which the Ramblers' Association was founded in 1935, and for many ramblers the access legislation represents the achievement of literally a lifetime of campaigning.

So now, at last, we do have freedom to roam. For the first time in several centuries, the open mountains, moors and heaths of England and Wales are open for all. We have the protected right to get our boots wet in the peat bogs, to flounder in the tussocks, to blunder and scrabble through the bracken and heather, and to discover countryside which, legally, we had no way of knowing before.

The Freedom to Roam series of books has one aim: to encourage you to explore and grow to love these new areas of the countryside which are now open to us. The right to roam freely – that's surely something to celebrate.

Walking in open country – a guide to using this book

If the right and the freedom to roam openly are so important – perceptive readers may be asking – why produce a set of books to tell you where to go?

So a word of explanation about this series. The aim is certainly not to encourage walkers to follow each other, ant-like, over the hills, sticking rigidly to a pre-determined itinerary. We are not trying to be prescriptive, instructing you on your walk stile by stile or gate by gate. The books are not intended as instruction manuals but we hope that they will be valuable as *guides* – helping you discover areas of the countryside which you haven't legally walked on before, advising you on routes you might want to take and telling you about places of interest you will be passing along the way.

In area where it can be tricky to find routes or track down landmarks, we offer more detailed instructions.

Elsewhere, we are deliberately less precise in our directions, allowing you to choose your own particular path or line to follow. For each walk, however, there is a recommended core route, and this forms the basis on which the distances given are calculated.

There is, then, an assumption that those who use this book will be comfortable with using a map – and that, in practice, means one of the Ordnance Survey's 1:25 000 Explorer series of maps. As well as referring to the maps in this book, it is worth taking the full OS map with you, to give you a wider picture of the countryside you will be exploring.

Safety in the hills

Those who are already experienced upland walkers will not be surprised if at this point we put in a note on basic safety in the hills. Walkers need to remember that walking in open country, particularly high country, is different from footpath walking across farmland or more gentle countryside. The main risk for walkers is of being inadequately prepared for changes in the weather. Even in high summer, hail and even snow are not impossible. Daniel Defoe found this out in August 1724 when he crossed the Pennines from Rochdale, leaving a calm clear day behind to find himself almost lost in a blizzard on the tops.

If rain comes the temperature will drop as well, so it is important to be properly equipped when taking to the hills and to guard against the risk of hypothermia. Fortunately, walkers today have access to a range of wind- and rain-proof clothing which was not available in the eighteenth century. Conversely, in hot weather you should take sufficient water to avoid the risk of dehydration and hyperthermia (dangerous overheating of the body).

Be prepared for visibility to drop when (to use the local term) the clag descends on the hills. It is always sensible to take a compass. If you are unfamiliar with basic compass-and-map work, ask in a local outdoor equipment shop whether they have simple guides available or pick the brains of a more experienced walker.

The other main hazard, even for walkers who know the hills well, is that of suffering an accident such as a broken limb. If you plan to walk alone, it is sensible to let someone know in advance where you will be walking and when you expect to be back – the moorland and mountain rescue services which operate in the area covered by this book are very experienced but they are not psychic. Groups of walkers should tackle only what the least experienced or least fit member of the party can comfortably achieve. Take particular care if you intend to take children with you to hill country. And take a mobile phone by all means, but don't assume you can rely on it in an emergency, since some parts of the moors and hills will not pick up a signal. (If you can make a call and are in a real emergency situation, ring 999 – it is the police who co-ordinate mountain and moorland rescues.)

If this all sounds off-putting, that is certainly not the intention. The guiding principle behind the access legislation is that walkers will exercise their new-won rights with responsibility. Taking appropriate safety precautions is simply one aspect of acting responsibly.

Access land – what you can and can't do

The countryside which is covered by access legislation includes mountain, moor, heath, downland and common land. After the passing of the Countryside and Rights of Way Act 2000, a lengthy mapping process was undertaken, culminating in the production of 'conclusive' maps which identify land which is open for access. These maps (although not intended as guides for walking) can be accessed via the Internet, at www.countrysideaccess.gov.uk. Ordnance Survey maps

Note: Each walk has been graded, on a scale of 🥾 to 🥾🥾🥾🥾🥾, for the degree of difficulty involved. In general, walks are judged more difficult if they are (a) longer in mileage, and/or (b) involve more rough walking (across open moorland rather than on established footpaths), and/or (c) pose more navigational problems or venture into very unfrequented areas. But bear in mind that all the walks in this book require map-reading competence and some experience of hill walking.

published from 2004 onwards also show access land.

You can walk, run, birdwatch and climb on access land, although there is no new right to camp or to bathe in streams or lakes (or, of course, to drive vehicles). The regulations sensibly insist that dogs, where permitted, are on leads near livestock and during the bird-nesting season (1 March to 31 July). However, grouse moors have the right to ban dogs altogether, and in much of

the area covered by this book this is the case.

Access legislation also does not include the right to ride horses or bikes, though in some areas there may be pre-existing agreements that allow this. More information is available on the website given above and, at the time of writing, there is also an advice line on 0845 100 3298.

The access legislation allows for some open country to be permanently excluded from the right to roam. 'Excepted' land includes

Semer Water, Wensleydale

military land, quarries and areas close to buildings, and in addition landowners can apply for other open land to be excluded.

To the best of the authors' knowledge, all the walks in the Freedom to Roam series are either on legal rights of way or across access land included in the official 'conclusive' maps. However, you are asked to bear in mind that the books have been produced right at the start of the new access arrangements, before walkers have begun to walk the hills regularly and before any teething problems on the ground have been ironed out. As access becomes better established, it may be that minor changes to the routes suggested in these books will become appropriate or necessary. You are asked to remember that we are encouraging you to be flexible in the way you use these guides.

Walkers in open country also need to be aware that landowners have a further right to suspend or restrict access to their land for up to twenty-eight days a year. (In such cases of temporary closure there is normally still access on public holidays and on most weekends.) Notice of closure needs to be given in advance and the plan is that this information should be readily available to walkers, it is hoped at local information centres and libraries and also on the countryside access website and at popular entry points to access land. This sort of set-up has generally worked well in Scotland, where arrangements have been made to ensure that walkers in areas where deer hunting takes place can find out when and where hunting is happening.

Walkers will understand the sense in briefly closing small areas of open countryside when, for example, shooting is in progress (grouse shooting begins on 12 August) or when heather burning is taking place in spring. Once again, however, it is too early in the implementation of the access legislation to know how easily walkers in England and Wales will be able to find out about these temporary access closures. It is also too early to know whether landowners will attempt to abuse this power.

In some circumstances, additional restrictions on access can be introduced – for example, on the grounds of nature or heritage conservation, following the advice of English Nature or English Heritage.

Bear these points in mind, but enjoy your walking in the knowledge that any access restrictions should be the exception and not the norm. If you find access unexpectedly denied while walking in the areas suggested in this book, please accept the restrictions and follow the advice you are given. However, if you feel that access was wrongly denied, please report your experience to the countryside service of the local authority (or national park authority, in national park areas) and to the Ramblers' Association.

Finally, there may be occasions when you choose voluntarily not to exercise your freedom to roam. For example, many of the upland moors featured in these books are the homes of ground-nesting birds such as grouse, curlew, lapwing and pipit, who will be nesting in spring and early summer. During this time, many people will decide to leave the birds in peace and find other places to walk. Rest assured that you will know if you are approaching an important nesting area – birds are good at telling you that they would like you to go away.

Celebrating the open countryside

Despite these necessary caveats, the message from this series is, we hope, clear. Make the most of the new legal rights we have been given – and enjoy your walking.

Introduction

Q Which is the most beautiful of the Yorkshire Dales?

A Swaledale

Wainwright, famous for his books on the Lakeland fells but also in his time a seasoned walker in the Dales, was never one to feel the need to avoid controversy. When he came out with this bald assertion (it was made in his *Pennine Way Companion*), he would probably have relished the idea that he might be stirring up debate and disagreement among others who love the Yorkshire Dales.

Yes, Swaledale – the debate might go – is certainly a very beautiful dale. But surely there are other claimants for the top prize? What about Dentdale, perhaps? The upper reaches of Wharfedale beyond Kettlewell? Maybe Nidderdale, excluded from the Dales national park but still most definitely one of the Yorkshire Dales? What of Walden or Coverdale, two of the set of beautiful valleys which feed in to Wensleydale from the south? For that matter, what about Wensleydale itself, wider and busier than Swaledale admittedly but for those who know it full of history and interest?

How can we begin to judge the attractions of one Yorkshire dale against another? And, frankly, why even begin an exercise like this? The point, surely, is that the Yorkshire Dales are, collectively, one of the most loved stretches of countryside in Britain – in the words of the national park authority, one of the finest upland areas of Britain and just the place to come for inspiration and relaxation. There would surely be few people who wouldn't agree with this statement at least.

And yet turn the clock back, say, a hundred and fifty years and this sort of assertion would have seemed in many ways very peculiar, certainly to those who lived and worked in the

Dales. Take Wainwright's favourite dale, Swaledale, for example. This was hardly the place to visit for peace and quiet, not unless you chose where you went very carefully to avoid the great sweeps of country on both sides of the dale where mining was under way. Swaledale and Arkengarthdale and Wensleydale, too, were to a considerable extent industrial areas. The natural features of the landscape were changed and moulded to allow access to the riches below the soil.

Coal has been taken from the earth of the northern Yorkshire Dales, particularly from the coalfield at the head of Arkengarthdale near Tan Hill, for centuries. In medieval times it was coal from Tan Hill which was burned in many northern fireplaces and records of Tan Hill coal go back to the late 1200s. But it was mining for lead, the dominant activity in much of the area covered by this book, which has left the most profound mark on the landscape in this part of the Dales.

The story of lead mining here goes back for close to two millennia and possibly even longer. We know that the Romans came to the Pennines in search of lead because a number of lead pigs (ingots) with Roman inscriptions have been found. One pig was reportedly discovered in an old Roman mine working at Hurst Bank in Swaledale, which was unexpectedly opened up by miners during the nineteenth century (the pig has unfortunately not survived, so the story is difficult to confirm).

The easiest way to get lead ore out of the ground is simply to remove it at the points where the mineral veins break the surface, or to dig shallow trenches which follow the lines of the veins. Unfortunately, all the lead which could be obtained in this way was removed in the very earliest days of lead mining. It was the Romans who began the process of extending the search for lead underground.

In the heyday of lead mining in the Dales, from the sixteenth to the nineteenth centuries, other techniques were used. One effective process was called hushing. This involved building a turf dam to hold water in a temporary reservoir at the head of a steep valley; when the dam was broken a torrent of water was released to rush down the hillside, carrying away the topsoil and loose rocks and exposing any mineral veins beneath. Once found, veins could then be worked by quarrying, with hushing used only periodically to flush away debris.

Hushing was a clever idea, although unfortunately for us today it involved some major interference with the countryside. While much of the underground and surface remains of lead mining in the northern Dales have been absorbed back into the landscape and may go unnoticed by casual visitors, the hushes, such as those that took place along the eastern side of Gunnerside Beck (Walk 6), left a much more stark reminder of the area's mining past.

Hushing was only one way of extracting lead ore. To get to ore lying deeper below the surface required the sinking of shafts, to ever-increasing depths. Deep shafts could access ore which had been previously out of reach, but they suffered two drawbacks: a potential lack of ventilation and the permanent risk of flooding. The solution, developed in Britain from as early as the fourteenth century although introduced into the lead-mining industry in the Dales rather later, was to drive levels into the hillside to meet up with existing underground shafts. A level could be started much lower down the hillside and could therefore act as a conduit to drain off unwanted water from the bottom of the shaft.

Near Hawes, Wensleydale

In the later years of the lead-mining industry, the levels were impressive engineering feats in their own right, laid with railway tracks and built high and wide enough that horses could pull trucks laden with lead ore through the Pennine hills. Walk the hills and valleys of the northern Yorkshire dales today and the entrances to these levels are not difficult to discover. The extensive network of tunnels and workings is now being rediscovered by both cavers and industrial archaeologists (often in practice the same people). In particular, the commendable Northern Mine Research Society has done much to ensure that this important aspect of northern England's industrial history is adequately recorded for posterity.

The shafts and levels which represent the underground part of the lead-mining industry are matched by remains which can be found on the surface. Lead didn't arrive above ground, of course, with the ore neatly sorted in a form ready for smelting. The valuable lead ore came up mixed with rock and other minerals, most of which were of little or no commercial value to the miners. They called this mix of other minerals gangue, and one of the first tasks on the surface was to sort the lead ore from the gangue.

This work was called dressing and it took place on so-called dressing floors. Water was the key here, because lead ore is heavy and conveniently sinks to the bottom when sifted in water with other minerals – in the same way as gold does during panning. To be able to separate lead ore in this way required a water supply, and moorland streams which could be diverted to feed into dressing floors were valuable assets. Fortunately, the Dales moors are not short of water.

First, however, considerable human effort had to be expended to break the large lumps of lead, gangue and clay which had emerged from the mines into fine particles which could be sorted effectively. Worthless rock could be quickly disposed of on a waste heap, but mixed lead ore and rock had to be broken down by hammering. Later on, particularly in the nineteenth century, this task was made easier in larger mines by the use of waterwheel-powered rock crushers, but for much of the history of lead mining in the Pennines the task of wielding the hammers fell to human beings, usually to boys who were given employment on the dressing floors after they reached the age of about eleven or twelve. Women, too, worked on the dressing floors.

This was not only hard physical work, it was also work which had to be undertaken in the full teeth of whatever weather came across the high hills. Walkers today who find themselves on the Swaledale or Wensleydale hills in bad conditions should perhaps take off their modern waterproofs and spend several hours in the rain hammering rocks together, to get a sense of dressing-floor work – although this is not a heritage experience which the tourist industry is likely to want to develop.

Once lead ore had been separated from rock and gangue minerals, the next stage was smelting, a process which involved subjecting the ore to intense heat and then casting the molten lead into ingots. Most of the mines or groups of mines in the Yorkshire Dales had their own smelt mills, typically close to the dressing floors. Many of these, now in ruins, are still there on the moors, testimony to the past industrial age.

Lead mining on any scale disappeared from the Dales during the later years of the nineteenth century, which means that now, more than a century on, this important chapter in the life of the area has effectively disappeared from collective memory. It now takes reading and research to get a real understanding of how the industry functioned. To appreciate what it was like, at a human level, to earn your livelihood from lead can be even more difficult. But perhaps a song can help.

The folk-singer Ewan MacColl has already been mentioned in this book, in the context of his anthem to the access movement, 'The Manchester Rambler' (see page 7). Shortly after the Second World War, MacColl, together with his then partner Joan Littlewood, met with a retired lead miner, John Gowland, and collected from him a powerful song describing the life of a young boy working on the dressing floor. 'Fourpence a Day' is believed to have been written by Thomas Raine, a Teesdale poet who was himself a lead miner. One, perhaps apocryphal, story has it that mine owners were so incensed when they heard the song that they closed the mines and dismissed their workers. The song certainly doesn't pull its punches and although (as its dialect demonstrates) it originates from the lead-mining area slightly to the north of the region covered in this book, a verse or two surely deserve repeating:

The ore is waiting in the tubs, the snow's upon the fell;
Canny folk are sleeping yet, but lead is reet to sell.
Come, my little washer lad, come let's away,
We're bound down to slavery for fourpence a day.

It's early in the morning, we rise at five o'clock,
And the little slaves come to the door to knock, knock, knock.
Come, my little washer lad, come let's away.
It's very hard to work for fourpence a day.

Here, then, is one aspect of the story of the northern Dales, to take its place with those other strands of history which, perhaps, are more immediately associated with tourism: the Romans at Bainbridge, the monks at Jervaulx Abbey, Mary Queen of Scots at Bolton Castle, and the like. In fact, history of all kinds will be encountered by those who undertake the walks in this book. There are prehistoric cup-marked rocks (Walk 2) and a curious 'banjo' hill fort to explore (Walk 5). There is a chance to follow the route the Romans took from Wharfedale into Wensleydale (Walk 1). There is the opportunity to ponder the fate of the Knights Templar, in their day the Church's most powerful order of soldier-monks, at the ruins of their chapel in the peaceful Wensleydale fields below Pen Hill (Walk 3). The bleak high moorland track taken by the formidable Lady Anne Clifford during her journeys through the Dales in the seventeenth century forms a part of another route (Walk 12). And, certainly, there are walks which explore the old lead-mining and coal-mining areas of the northern Dales, passing the levels, the old smelt mills and the ruins of the dressing floors where, once upon a time, the ore would be waiting in the tubs on the cold fells for the washer lads to arrive.

This rich history adds to the enjoyment and satisfaction which comes from getting to know this part of Yorkshire. Whether or not you want to argue with Wainwright for the particular delights of Swaledale, you will almost certainly agree with Alf Wight who, better known as the vet James Herriot, spoke with love and passion about the high country of these northern Dales. 'It is up there on the empty moors with the curlews crying that I have been able to find peace and tranquillity of mind,' he wrote once.

James Herriot was fortunate in being able to work in a beautiful landscape. For those of us living in urban areas, getting to know the Dales may have to be fitted in at weekends or holiday times, a journey of exploration which can take a lifetime. And now, since 2005 when access legislation was first implemented in the Dales, there is so much more to explore. Astonishingly, the area of the Yorkshire Dales National Park that is open to walkers to explore as of right has increased from 4 per cent before the Countryside and Rights of Way Act to about 63 per cent today. The walks in this book willingly make use of the network of footpaths and bridleways where appropriate; but where appropriate, too, they make for the open hills.

Muker from Kisdon Hill, Swaledale

WALK 1

DODD FELL

DIFFICULTY 👟👟👟   **DISTANCE 11 miles (17.5 km)**

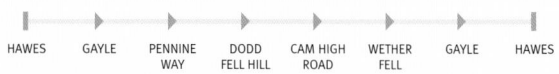

| HAWES | GAYLE | PENNINE WAY | DODD FELL HILL | CAM HIGH ROAD | WETHER FELL | GAYLE | HAWES |

MAP OS Explorer OL30, Yorkshire Dales (Northern and Central) or Harveys Dales South

STARTING POINT Hawes (GR 873898)

PUBLIC TRANSPORT There are buses from Northallerton and Leyburn (which also continue to Gayle) and connecting buses for some trains at Garsdale station (not Sundays). Services run from Leeds, Wakefield, Darlington, Kettlewell and Skipton on summer Sundays/Bank Holidays (more limited winter services also currently run). Other local services operate.

PARKING In one of the car parks in Hawes

A delightful horseshoe route around Sleddale, south of Hawes. Mostly track and footpath walking. About 1 mile (1.6 km) of rough open country over Dodd Fell.

▸ Take the road (with a footpath sign for Gayle Lane) beside Hawes church, to pick up the footpath which runs across fields to Gayle. Alternatively, start the walk at Gayle.

■ The path skirts the Wensleydale dairy (see

page 36). The story of the production of Wensleydale cheese in Hawes is closely linked to that of Kit Calvert, a local man who was almost single-handedly responsible for keeping cheese making alive in upper Wensleydale in the mid-twentieth century. The first cheese factory in Hawes was opened in 1898 by Edward Chapman, but by 1935 the dairy was in trading difficulties and facing closure. Kit Calvert, who farmed near by and who was well known locally as, among other things, a lay preacher (he translated part of the Bible into Wensleydale dialect), called a meeting in the Town Hall and gathered enough support to rescue the dairy. He went on to become the dairy's managing director and oversaw the move to the current Gayle Lane site in 1953.

▸ Follow the Pennine Way as it threads its way through the houses on the outskirts of Gayle (or walk to the main junction in the village and turn right). Once past Rookhurst Hotel, look for the P.W. footpath sign on your left and follow the Pennine Way across fields to pick up the start of Gaudy Lane ❶. (It ought to be easy to follow the route of Britain's premier long-distance trail. However, the route of the Pennine Way here is not entirely straightforward. Take care not to end up on the footpath near Gayle Beck.)

Once past Gaudy House farm, the Pennine Way becomes a delightful green path, climbing steadily. After 2 miles (3 km) or so, the path is met by the stony Cam Road coming up from the right. Carry on until you reach the open moor ❷.

At an appropriate point, leave the Pennine Way to head up across the grass towards the summit of Dodd Fell Hill ❸. With luck, faint trods can be found heading in the right direction.

■ The walk out on the Pennine Way has been dominated by the view, almost due south ahead, of the unmistakable shape of Penyghent. As you climb Dodd Fell, the views become

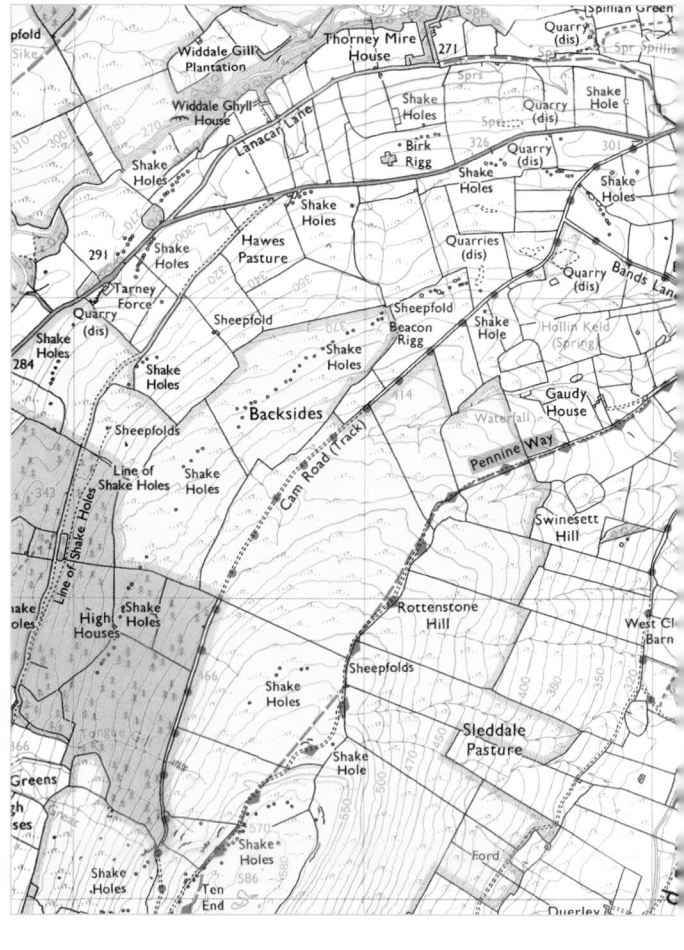

more extensive. Whernside is to the south-west, while further away is the high ground of Calf Top, near Dent.

Equally attractive is the view back down Sleddale to the town of Hawes, lying in the valley below.

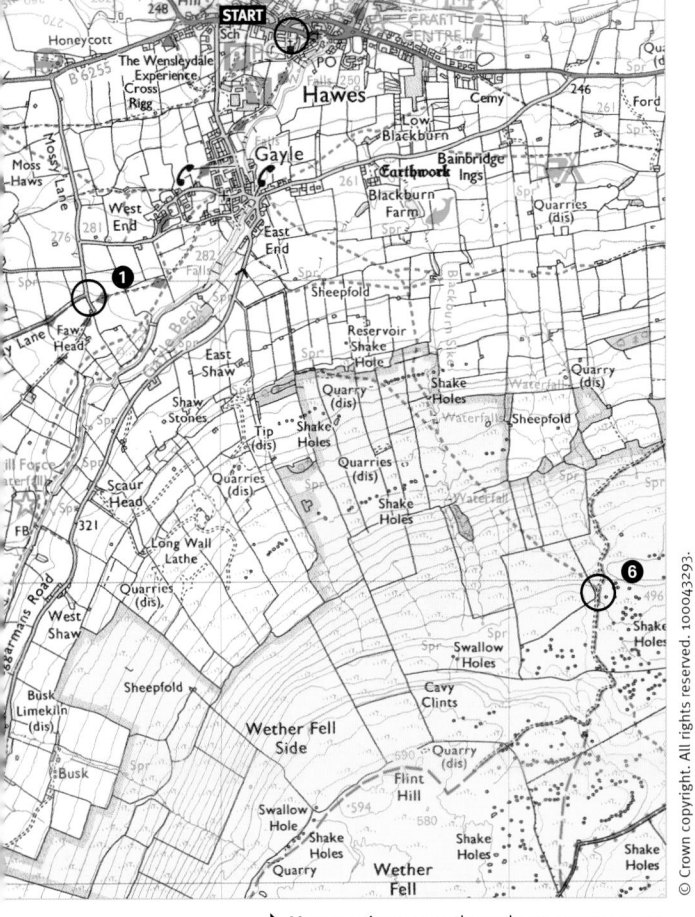

▶ Map continues southwards on pages 30–31

Dodd Fell Hill is not quite as significant a mountain as Whernside or Penyghent, but nevertheless it still manages a very respectable 2191 ft (668 m). Passed by the Pennine Way to the west (and not crossed by any rights of way), it has been unfairly neglected in the past by walkers.

▸ Beyond Dodd Fell Hill top, an initially promising path heading east rapidly disappears in very

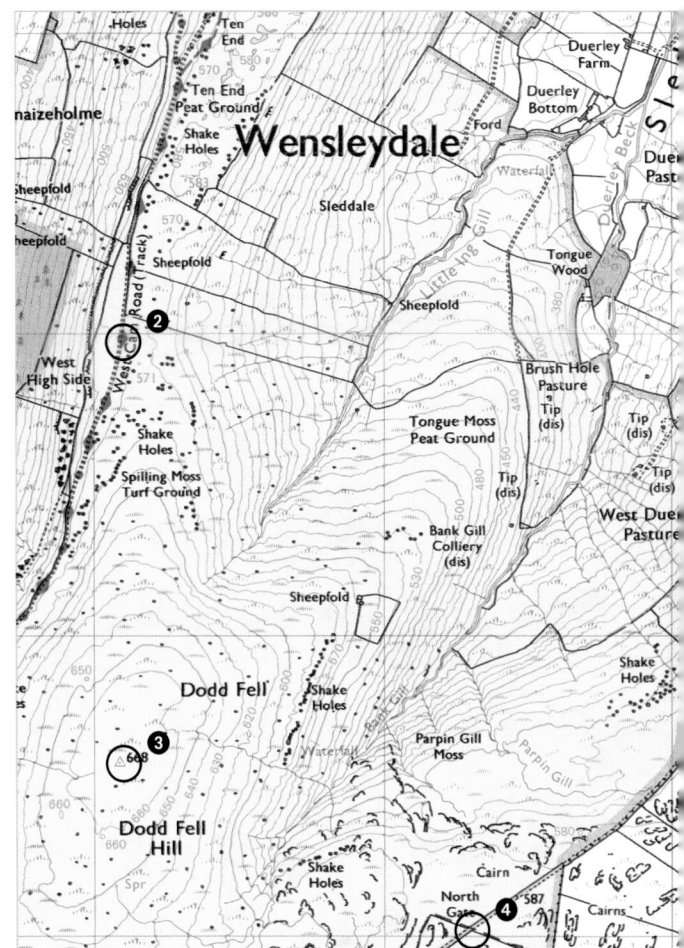

wet ground. Aim south-eastwards, to avoid the upper reaches of Bank Gill river. This can be rough walking, but eventually you will reach Cam High Road, the metalled road to Cam Houses.

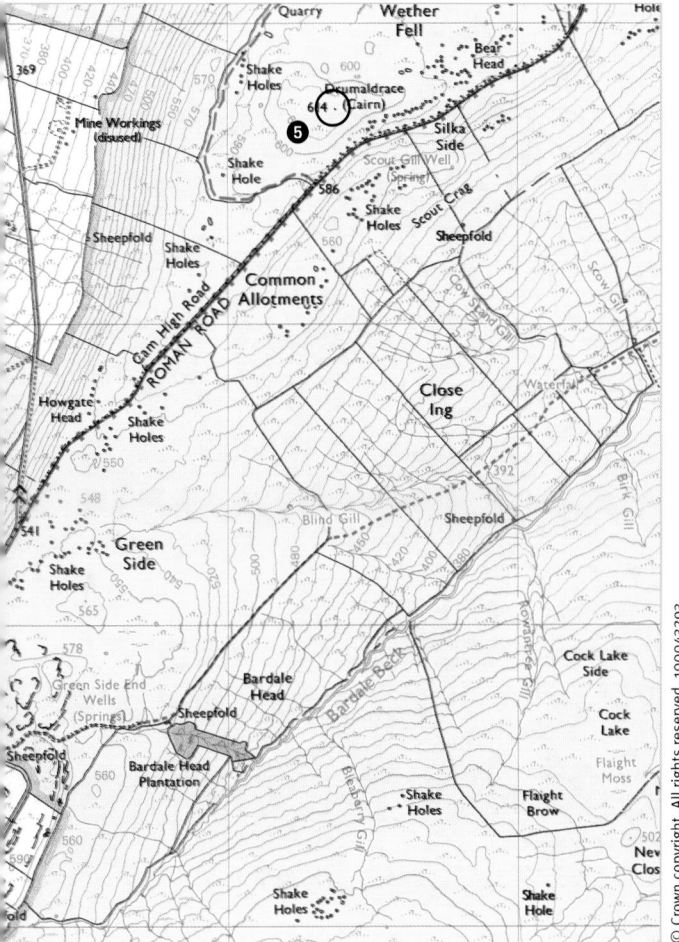

Aim to leave the moor at North Gate ❹.

■ From here, the walk picks up one of the most historic routes across these fells, first used two thousand years ago when the Romans came to occupy the area. As a cursory glance at the OS map reveals, the Cam High Road runs in an almost straight line north-eastwards, making directly for Brough Hill outside Bainbridge where the Romans constructed a fort. This fort, known to the Romans as Virosidum, has been the subject of extensive excavations by the University of Leeds.

The line of the Roman road is also easy to trace in the other direction, first to Gearstones in upper Ribblesdale and then, still in a more-or-less straight line, along the modern B6255 past Chapel-le-Dale to Ingleton. Beyond Ingleton, the eventual destination for the road seems to have been Lancaster, although the route is much less obvious on the ground.

The line of the Roman road was chosen in the mid-eighteenth century for the Richmond–Lancaster turnpike road. The turnpike, 60 miles (95 km) in total, was authorized in 1751 and followed the line originally established by the Romans south from Bainbridge. However, at the end of the eighteenth century the route was changed, to follow the modern road through Hawes and then up Widdale to Gearstones. The new turnpike route only involved a climb out of Wensleydale to about 1435 ft (438 m) at the head of Widdale, compared with the climb to almost 1950 ft (600 m) necessary on the Roman road.

▸ Continue on Cam High Road to the junction with the Hawes–Kettlewell road. At this point, it's possible to cross over and make your way northwards over open ground parallel to the road; alternatively, follow the road briefly. In either case, the Cam High Road quickly ceases to carry modern traffic and reverts to being a stony track. Follow it north-eastwards, to reach the open moorland of Wether Fell. Over to the right, there's a pleasant view down to Semer Water with Addlebrough beyond (Walk 2).

Climb up to the cairn at the top of Wether Fell ❺, and continue across the fell to join the bridleway which runs along the western edge of the open ground. Leave Wether Fell by the gate at the north end, picking up the bridleway which hurries down the hillside, heading almost due north. Shortly after passing a shed, look for the start of a footpath ❻ which leaves the bridleway to head back to Gayle.

From here, it's a delightful descent through fields with Gayle and Hawes directly below. The footpath ends in the heart of Gayle village, opposite Gayle Mill.

■ Gayle Mill briefly attracted national attention in the summer of 2004, when it was a runner-up in BBC2's heritage programme *Restoration*. Unfortunately, Gayle Mill's third place in the competition was not enough to enable the North East Civic Trust, which now owns the building, to receive any additional grant funding to help restore the mill, but it did at least serve to galvanize local support.

The mill was built in 1776 by the Rouths, an old Wensleydale family, and it was one of the first mechanized cotton mills in the area. The mill was powered by a waterwheel, and the leat (channel) from Gayle Beck to the mill is a prominent feature today.

In the early nineteenth century, Gayle Mill appears to have changed from cotton to spinning flax and then, later still, to wool. Hawes and Gayle were already long-established centres of the hand-knitting industry. George Walker, whose 1814 book *The Costume of Yorkshire* is now considered a classic, wrote of the importance of knitting in the area: 'Young and old, male and female, all are adapts in this art.'

In the late 1870s, Gayle Mill was converted into a saw mill and the waterwheel was replaced by a turbine. The North East Civic Trust say that the early woodworking machinery installed at this time is also of historical importance. The mill building itself is protected, as a Grade II* Listed Building.

The work of fundraising to restore the mill continues, but, after a period in the late twentieth century when

the fabric of the building was allowed to decay and its future was in doubt, Gayle Mill is now in a better state than for many years. Despite not winning the BBC competition, the Gayle Mill story seems likely to end happily.

▸ Return from Gayle to Hawes town centre.

Hawes, Wensleydale

Cheese making in the Dales

Wensleydale, one of the traditional cheeses of England, nearly disappeared from its Yorkshire home for good in 1992. Dairy Crest, the then-owners of the Hawes creamery, were rationalizing their cheese-making empire and announced that their manufacture of Wensleydale would in future take place across the great divide, in Lancashire. There was campaigning, there was lobbying, but in May that year the creamery closed taking with it fifty-nine jobs, a massive economic blow for Hawes and the communities near by.

But there is a happy ending to the story. After six months of darkness the creamery reopened, this time with a local management team in charge. The first batch of the new, 'real' Wensleydale cheeses was ready for Christmas that year.

It's been a famous success story since then, of course, helped by some adroit marketing and the contribution of well-known Wensleydale cheese-lovers Wallace and Gromit. As well as producing traditional cheese using milk from cows grazed in the upper dale, the company has also added a ewes' milk Wensleydale to its range and has begun manufacturing other classic cheeses such as Red Leicester and Double Gloucester. The milk for Hawes is collected daily by tankers which make a circuit of farms in upper Wensleydale (all within ten miles of the dairy), and it is this emphasis on local milk from cows grazing on Dales limestone which, the company claims, gives the cheeses their particular quality and taste. Every day, 28,000 litres of milk arrive at Hawes to be transformed into cheese.

The cheese making is paramount, according to Alice Amsden, production director at Wensleydale Dairy Products, but the company has also developed a successful visitors' centre where the public can view the cheese being made (and of course

Making Wensleydale cheese at Hawes

purchase it afterwards). In a further expansion in 2000, the company acquired the former Fountains Dairy at Kirkby Malzeard near Ripon, so in total around 170 people now earn their livelihood from the business.

It's been a similar story of growth, albeit on a smaller scale, at the Swaledale Cheese company, a family business run by David and Mandy Reed and now located in Richmond. The Reeds produce a range that attempts to recreate the traditional tastes of Swaledale cheeses. Cows' milk, ewes' milk and goats' milk cheeses are all produced, as well as an organic Swaledale made from milk from a single farm in Low Row, upper Swaledale.

The renewed public interest in locally made quality cheeses is welcome, but the fact remains that the tradition of farmhouse cheese making which used to be such an important part of Dales life has, sadly, disappeared for good. As with other aspects of British cuisine, the Second World War took a heavy toll. At the start of the war, according to Bill Mitchell, the former *Dalesman* editor, cheese was regularly made in more than a hundred farmhouses up and down the Dales. By the end of the war, however, only six farmhouse cheese makers were left. The problem was that traditional Wensleydale cheese was moist and crumbly while wartime rationing rules required cheeses to be harder, to ensure that the small portions which could be claimed on ration cards weren't too full of moisture. A tradition which went back centuries came to an abrupt end.

The tale as it's generally recounted is that cheese making was brought to the Yorkshire Dales from France by the monks at Jervaulx in lower Wensleydale. These early Wensleydale cheeses would have been made from ewes' milk and would probably have turned blue naturally, through a similar process to that still used today to make Roquefort cheese in France. After the Dissolution of the Monasteries cheese making carried on at farmhouse level until the middle of the nineteenth century, when the first modern cheese creamery was opened in

Wensleydale. The Hawes dairy can trace its roots back beyond the days of Dairy Crest to 1897, when a local merchant began to purchase milk in bulk from farmers in the area to manufacture cheese on a more commercial scale.

Modern Wensleydale may seem to us today a familiar and long-established English cheese, but it bears little resemblance to the farmhouse Wensleydales which were produced before the Second World War. One of the few people to try to recreate the traditional taste of Wensleydale is Suzanne Stirke of Fortmayne Farm Dairy in Newton-le-Willows near Bedale, and yet, ironically, contemporary regulations prevent her from giving the cheese she sells the Wensleydale tag – instead she has opted for the name King Richard III. The story she tells is that, after deciding to set up her cheese-making business fifteen or so years ago, she stumbled almost by chance on some old books from the 1930s which had been acquired by her grandmother and subsequently banished to the attic, and which to her delight gave recipes for making traditional Wensleydale cheese. Suzanne used these old recipes to help her devise her own cheese. Much of her produce now goes to London to be sold at outlets such as Fortnum and Mason, although fortunately for Yorkshire residents and visitors a small amount makes the much shorter journey to a delicatessen in Masham.

If it's encouraging that one very small producer is continuing to offer a farmhouse Wensleydale, it's also disappointing that, because of the way that cheese production is now controlled, Suzanne Stirke has had to give up making cheeses from unpasteurized milk and stop producing her own ewes' milk cheese. It simply wasn't possible, she says, to find time to milk the ewes herself or to find a suitable high-quality source of ewes' milk elsewhere, as regulations now require. And she warns other would-be cheese makers that the task of meeting modern regulations can be onerous. Farmhouse cheese making today is, she says, 'almost impossible'.

WALK 2

ADDLEBROUGH

DIFFICULTY 👟 👟 **DISTANCE** 5½ miles (9 km)

WORTON   THORNTON RUST MOOR   ADDLEBROUGH   WORTON

MAP OS Explorer OL30, Yorkshire Dales (Northern and Central) or Harveys Dales North

STARTING POINT Worton, on the road between Bainbridge and Aysgarth (GR 956900)

PUBLIC TRANSPORT Buses from Northallerton, Leyburn and Hawes

PARKING In the lay-by at the Aysgarth end of the village

A relatively short walk across moors to the impressive summit of Addlebrough. A short section of walking across open ground.

▶ Leave Worton, walking along the main road in the direction of Aysgarth. Shortly after passing the pub, take the footpath on the right which meanders its way up the hillside towards Thornton Rust.

■ After leaving Worton the footpath runs close to a number of drumlins, oval-shaped hillocks made of boulder clay and pebbles, which were laid down and shaped in the glacial period by passing ice sheets as they moved through the valley. Wensleydale is a classic

U-valley, the creation (as every geography textbook will note) of glacial activity.

The footpath to Thornton Rust from Worton offers a study in stiles, since the path takes apparent wanton delight in choosing a route which involves the crossing of as many field walls as possible. The reason, of course, is that the walls are a later addition to the landscape – the path was here first.

▶ Turn right in the centre of Thornton Rust ❶, passing the car parking area. Take the track beyond as it climbs up the hillside. Turn left ❷ at the bridleway sign and follow the bridleway across the open land of Thornton Rust Moor. Continue until you reach a sign for the concessionary path to Addlebrough on your right ❸.

■ Addlebrough is at its most impressive when approached from this side. Until access legislation was implemented in the Dales in 2005, the concessionary path was the only means of reaching the top of the hill.

▶ The footpath runs across the moor, climbing up the flank of Addlebrough. The summit plateau ❹ is reached by a ladder stile.

■ Addlebrough no longer has its own trig point (it was removed when Ordnance Survey ceased to need the country's triangulation network of trig points for map making), but a modern cairn near by acts as a suitable substitute.

It's worth walking along the summit to the west side of the plateau, to enjoy the view down to Raydale and, particularly, to Semer Water. Semer Water is one of only two natural lakes within the Yorkshire Dales area, the other being Malham Tarn to the south. Both were created by glacial erosion, which scoured out hollows that later became lakes held in by natural dams of moraine material (or in other words by the earth, stones and rocks carried by glaciers).

Semer Water is best known for the tale of the lost city said to lie in its depths. Every guidebook, it seems, has to recount Yorkshire's answer to the Sodom and Gomorrah legend. The story goes that there was once a rich city here whose inhabitants failed to provide hospitality to a poor traveller who came this way. He extracted his revenge by cursing the city and causing it to be flooded.

Despite the story, there is no city to be uncovered in the shallow bottom of Semer Water. It is possible, however, that there were settlements there in prehistoric times which were subsequently flooded. Early human history is, in any case, close at hand in this area. A number of prehistoric sites have been identified on the slopes of Addlebrough, and the hill is also remarkable for its examples of prehistoric rock art.

Rock art of the cup-and-ring and cup-mark kind is particularly associated with Rombalds Moor near Ilkley,

where there is an astonishing concentration of rock carvings, including highly complex designs. The Freedom to Roam guide *South Pennines and the Bronte Moors* includes a

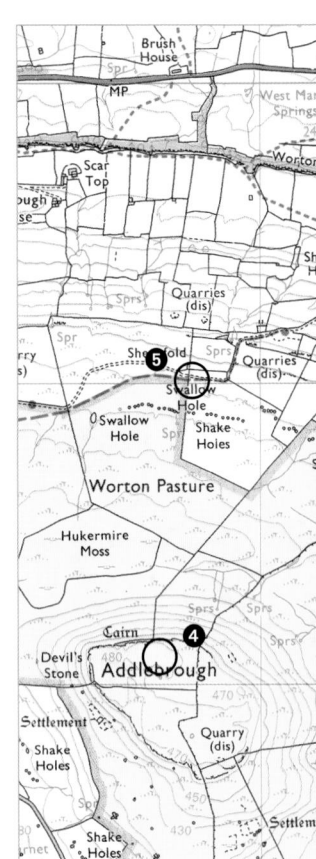

detailed account of the rock art on Rombalds Moor, featuring two walks which visit a number of examples.

Nowhere else in Britain can match the Ilkley area for the number of rock carvings, but nevertheless similar prehistoric cup and cup-and-ring stones have been found in many other parts of the country, including

▶ page 46

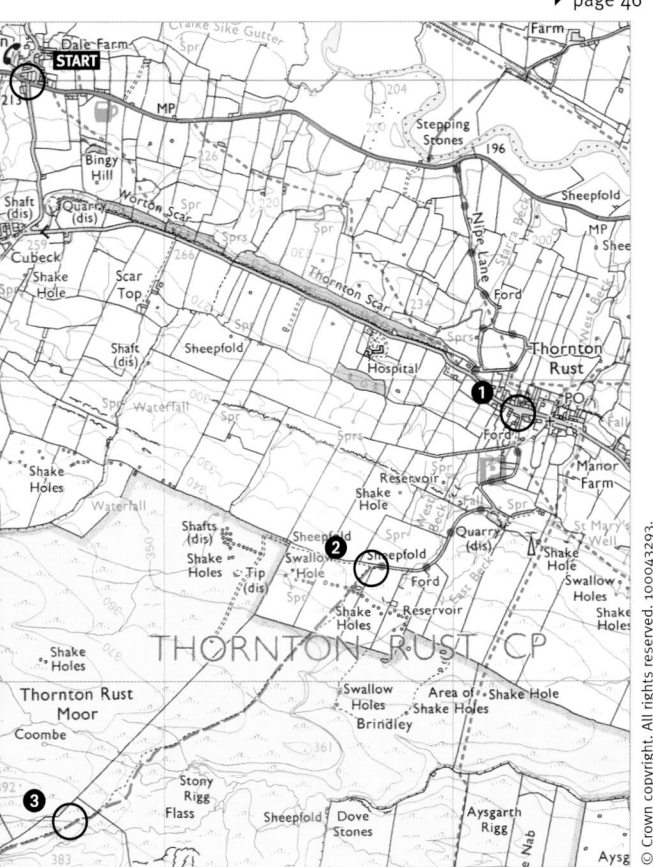

Askrigg, Wensleydale, with Addlebrough in the distance

Dartmoor, Snowdonia, Anglesey, the Isle of Man, Perthshire, Argyll and the Scottish borders. Small but significant numbers of carved rocks have been found on the North York Moors, and in the Dales examples have come to light in Swaledale and Wensleydale, as well as in Nidderdale and Wharfedale, closer to Ilkley.

Some archaeologists are anxious that the Addlebrough examples should not be publicized too widely, since unfortunately vandalism has occurred here in the past. For this reason, your author at this point will exercise a certain discretion and will fail to give precise directions. However, it is fair to say that the four cup-marked rocks (one of which also has a simple ring) will not be difficult to discover by those who visit Addlebrough's summit plateau.

Another rock with several cup marks can also be found to the east of Addlebrough, on Thornton Rust Moor near the Dove Stones.

▶ Since 2005, it has been possible to leave Addlebrough to the north, dropping down the little gully near the cairn. As you head down the hill, use an existing partial gap in the fell wall to cross to the enclosure to your left. Lower down, another partial break in the fell wall gives access to Worton Pasture. (It would be helpful, now that this is access land, if these crossings could be properly equipped with stiles.) Cross Worton Pasture to find the bridleway at the bottom **5**.

Turn right and follow the lane back down, until you reach the Worton–Thornton Rust minor road. Continue on the road back to Worton.

Wensleydale Railway

The train currently waiting at the platform at Hawes railway station is not going anywhere in a hurry. Marooned on a short section of track, the engine looks ahead towards six miles of overgrown trackbed which snakes its lonely way alongside the upper reaches of the River Ure. At the other end of the platform are twelve more miles of ex-railway, including a missing river bridge and a bulldozed former embankment. Hawes station, and the train which it accommodates, are now nothing more than exhibits in the Dales Countryside Museum.

But a local action group is determined to dream the seemingly impossible and to get a real railway back to this part of the Yorkshire Dales. The 3500-strong Wensleydale Railway Association has the audacious aim not simply of creating a heritage line for tourists but of putting rails back through the Wensleydale valley as an integral part of the national rail network. And, against the odds, they have already been able to demonstrate that they're deadly serious.

The valley railway was built between 1848 and 1878 and in its day was a valuable through route, linking the east-coast main line at Northallerton with the Settle–Carlisle main line at Garsdale Head. But through passenger trains ran only until 1954. In the years after that, local passenger services were also removed, much of the track was ripped up and the trackbed itself was sold off. Stations like those at Hawes, Wensley and Aysgarth were closed. Only in the east did an amputated stump of the old line remain: twenty-two miles of track continued in use as a freight line to the quarry at Redmire, on the very boundary of the national park near Bolton Castle.

The 1980s were dominated by a campaign waged by the Ramblers' Association and the local community to save the Settle–Carlisle line and to reopen the intermediate stations for passenger trains. It was a hard-fought battle, but in the end it was successful and (for the time being at least) the line is off the danger list. By 1990, therefore, some of those active in that campaign had time to turn their attention elsewhere. A public meeting held in May that year at Hawes rekindled the vision of a railway through Wensleydale, which would once more make a trans-Pennine link through the heart of the Dales.

Ruth Annison, who with her husband runs the Outhwaite rope works in Hawes, was the inspiration for that meeting, and she has remained a key player in the Wensleydale Railway story. What motivates her is not so much the charm of steam engines puffing their way through the countryside; she talks instead of the need for rural economic regeneration and socially inclusive access to the countryside. Bringing back a railway to her dale isn't nostalgia, she insists, but rather a way of developing a sustainable transport infrastructure for the future.

The first battle in the embryonic campaign was to save the Redmire freight line, which was itself under threat of being closed down and sold off. The second aim was to reopen this section of the railway for passengers. With much effort, both these aims have been accomplished. The first trains, run by the newly created Wensleydale Railway plc, began operating from Leeming Bar (beside the A1 trunk road) to Leyburn in the summer of 2003. The company had to negotiate a formal operating licence with the national rail regulator and raise

£1.2 million in capital from members of the public. Fortunately, the new trains captured the public interest and since then, slowly, the service has been extended, in the west to Redmire and in the east towards the key town of Northallerton.

In 2004, Wensleydale Railway once again appealed to investors, this time for a further £2.75 million to help finance the next stage – bringing trains back to the disused section of trackbed. It's a big task: the eighteen miles between Garsdale and Redmire are now owned by about fifty separate landowners,

Trains are returning to Wensleydale

each of whom will have to be persuaded to sell or lease back their land. On top of that, the cost of re-laying railway track comes in at something over £1 million a mile.

But the Wensleydale Railway plans to take one step at a time. The next target is to extend the line beyond Redmire, past Castle Bolton and on to the town of Aysgarth. This will bring the railway to one of the most popular tourist destinations in the northern half of the national park – and, just as important, it will make the line more useful for local people wanting to get into and out of Wensleydale.

The focus is then likely to move to the other end of the valley, the aim being to bring trains once more down the mountainside into Hawes from the isolated station at Garsdale, allowing this moorland outpost of the railway network to reclaim its old name of Hawes Junction. At this stage, presumably, that train marooned in the Dales Countryside Museum will once again have somewhere to go. Finally, if all goes according to plan, the focus will switch to the last missing gap, the miles of derelict trackbed which in some ways are the biggest challenge of the lot.

It is, as Ruth Annison and her colleagues know, a major undertaking, one which they admit will take a generation to complete. But they are heartened by what they have managed to achieve so far. Indeed, their experience in Wensleydale has helped to create a model for rural railways in other parts of Britain, so that the government is now seriously looking at working in partnership with community-based groups to help keep the trains rolling. Of course, at a time when the long-term future of Britain's branch network remains uncertain, there's no guarantee that the lost link through Wensleydale will once again be shown on the railway maps. But if it comes down to sheer determination and energy, there may be a happy outcome yet.

WALK 3

PEN HILL

DIFFICULTY 🥾 🥾   **DISTANCE** 9¾ miles (15.7 km)

| WEST WITTON | PEN HILL | HAZELY PEAT MOOR | MORPETH SCAR | TEMPLARS' CHAPEL | REDMIRE FORCE | WEST WITTON |

MAP OS Explorer OL30, Yorkshire Dales (Northern and Central) or Harveys Dales North

STARTING POINT West Witton (GR 059884)

PUBLIC TRANSPORT Buses from Northallerton, Leyburn and Hawes

PARKING In the large lay-by at the Leyland end of the village

Fine views of Wensleydale from Pen Hill, followed by some riverside walking to the pleasant falls of Redmire Force.

■ West Witton, strung out along the A684, earns its place in guidebooks to the Yorkshire Dales as the village where, each year, the event known as the Burning of Bartle takes place.

This is one of those apparently inexplicable English folk traditions which continue year after year through sheer weight of history. In West Witton's case, it seems possible that Bartle – an effigy made, Guy Fawkes-like, of a head and body stuffed with straw – has been ceremoniously burned each year for four hundred years or more.

The event comes with its own rhyme, which West Witton children traditionally learned by heart by the time they were in primary school. The version recorded by Marie Hartley and Joan Ingilby in their 1956 book *The Yorkshire Dales* is as follows:

> In Penhill Crags he tore
>   his rags
> At Hunter's Thorn he blew
>   his horn
> At Capplebank Stee he
>   brake his knee
> At Grisgill Beck he brake
>   his neck
> At Wadham's End he
>   couldn't fend
> At Grisgill End he made
>   his end
> Shout lads shout.

As with all folk songs and rhymes, there is no official version cast in stone. A recent article in the *Dalesman* magazine suggested an alternative for the third line, 'At Capplebank Stee he 'appened [chanced] his fortune and brake his knee', and a slight variant for the penultimate line, 'At Grisgill End we'll mak his end'.

Either way, the rhyme appears to tell of the hunting of 'Bartle' from the height of Pen Hill above West Witton down the hillside and into the village. Local people have identified Hunter's Thorn as an old thorn bush below Pen Hill Scar, while Capple Bank, as modern maps show, is just to the south of the village. Grisgill is in West Witton itself.

So what, precisely, is the Burning of Bartle all about? Some have suggested a pagan origin, though folk memory in the village is that the event refers, rather gruesomely, to justice meted out in times past to a sheep stealer. True or otherwise, it is unlikely that the miscreant carried the name of Bartle. This part of the tradition almost certainly comes from the village's patron saint St Bartholomew, whose saint's day is 24 August. The Burning of Bartle takes place on the weekend nearest this date, as part of the West Witton Feast.

The Feast, West Witton's version of Bartholomew Fair, also has a long historical tradition and it continues to take place (after a shaky period a few years ago), with children's activities, sideshows and a fell race among the other attractions in addition to the parading and burning of Bartle himself.

▶ From West Witton, take the footpath which starts opposite the Wensleydale Heifer pub, heading up the hillside behind the village. Turn left when you reach High Lane, to join the by-road to Melmerby at Witton Steeps. A slightly quicker but less interesting route is simply to follow the by-road up from the village. Climb up the hill past Penhill Farm.

■ Opposite Penhill Farm are the Middleham High Moor gallops, used for exercising and training racehorses. Middleham, Yorkshire's answer to Newmarket, has several training stables and the area has been associated with racehorse breeding and

training for centuries. The turf of both Middleham High Moor and Middleham Low Moor (a little to the east) has long been pounded beneath horses' hooves, the High Moor traditionally being used as a summer gallop.

The link with horse breeding goes back to the monks of Jervaulx Abbey, who are known to have kept horses in Wensleydale in the twelfth century. At the time of the Dissolution of the Monasteries, the fine quality of the abbey's stallions and mares drew particular comment.

▶ Leave the minor road just beyond the gallops ❶, taking the bridleway towards Pen Hill. Follow the bridleway through a series of fields.

■ The boggy ground at the foot of Pen Hill marks the point where a spring emerges from the hillside. This is the spring which bears the name of Robin Hood's Well.

It is beginning to seem almost obligatory that books

▶ page 56

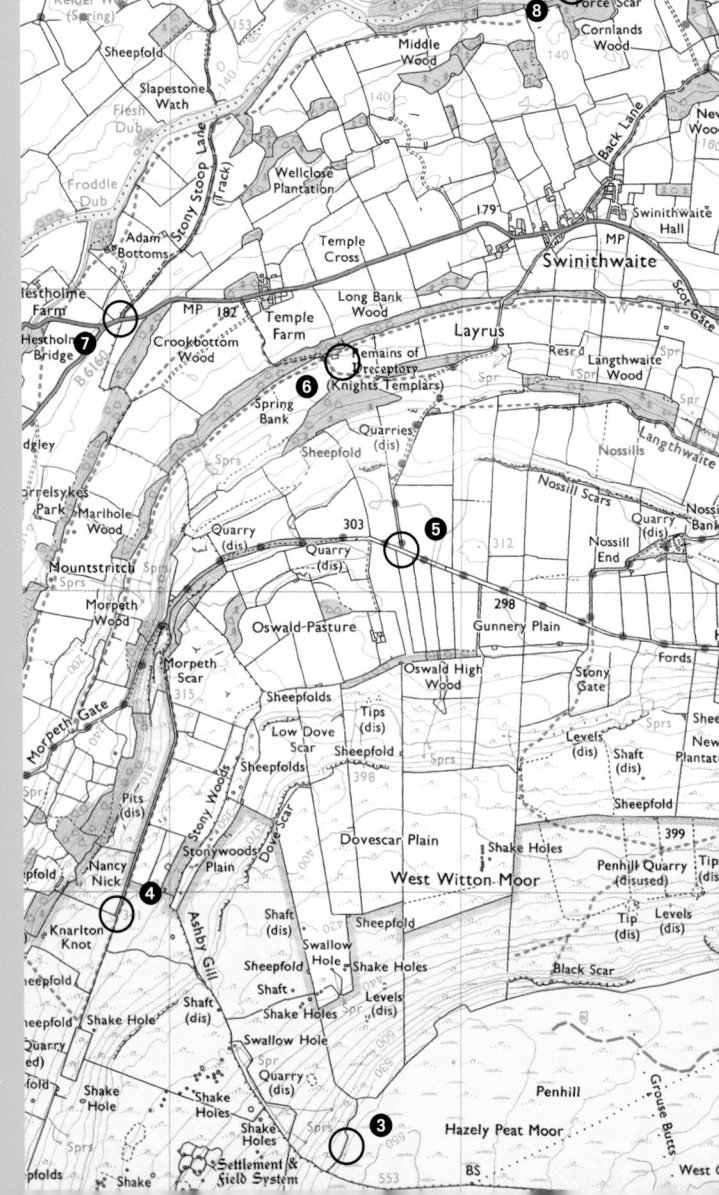

The Round

Haremire House

West Wood

East Haremire

FB

River Ure

Batt Island

High Wanlass

Wanlass Wath

Thickwood

Wanlass Park

Low Wanlass

Ice Pond

Sheepfold

164

Quarry (dis)

Sheepfold

Flats Lane

Lords Bridge

194

Mesnes Lane

WEST WITTON CP

MP 129

Alm Farm

Mesnes Plantation

Oak Tree Farm

Mill Beck

Sewage Works

Back Lane (Track)

Hollgate Plantation

Holl Gate

Bay Bolton Avenue

START

174

PO

West Witton

Wynbury

231

Kagram

Green Gate

Capple Bank Beck

High Wood

Chantry

Waterfall

212

Capple Bank Farm

Capple Bank

Quarry (dis)

Ford

Sheepfolds

Fords Tips (dis)

Witton Steeps

Tips (dis)

Capplebank Plant

Harrow Ridge

379

Sheepfolds

Tips (dis)

317

Penhill Farm

Middleham High

Sheepfolds

Flint Lane (Track)

Penhill Park

Tips (dis)

Swallow Hole

Shake Hole

1 BS

327

hill Crags

Scar

Penhill Beacon

2

Sheepfold

Cattle Grid

Wraykeld Well (Spring)

Robin Hood's Well (Spring)

Pile of Stones

BS

364

BS

Little Penhill

Shake Holes

East Gate

Fords

Level (dis)

Long Slack Quarry (disused)

334

Fords

Moss Slacks

Grouse butts

Brown Knots

Shake Holes

in the Freedom to Roam series include at least one visit to a spring allegedly associated with Robin Hood. This book's sister guide, *Wharfedale and Nidderdale*, suggests a walk to another Robin Hood's Well in the Yorkshire Dales, in that instance high on the hillside above Littondale. Those with the *Forest of Bowland* volume will find directions to a rather more famous Robin Hood's Well, on the flank of Pendle Hill in Lancashire. Its waters slaked the thirst of George Fox, the founder of the Quaker movement, after he clambered up the hill in 1652. Yet another Robin Hood's Well, this time near Haworth in West Yorkshire, features in the *South Pennines* volume. Robin Hood, evidently, was a man who frequently became thirsty.

In fact the name Robin is probably not a reference to the celebrated outlaw, but to the nature spirit Robin Goodfellow, who Shakespeare turned into the character Puck in *A Midsummer Night's Dream*. Springs and wells, as is well known, were often considered holy places.

Those who like to imagine that some of this pagan mystery still lingers may be interested to know that this particular Robin Hood's Well is (allegedly) located on several ley lines.

▶ Climb up the side of Pen Hill to the top. The map's dismissive 'pile of stones' hardly does justice to the care with which this particular hilltop creation has been made.

Continue along the hill edge, to the site of Pen Hill beacon ❷.

■ The tradition of lighting beacons on Pen Hill was maintained when a beacon was lit to celebrate the millennium. Pen Hill is also associated with a legend of a wicked giant who lived here, finally falling to his death from the crags.

▶ A path continues along the edge of Pen Hill Scar, offering fine views back to West Witton and Wensleydale below. (Visiting the trig point involves crossing the wall; to keep the best of the views, keep on the brow with the wall to your left.)

After a few hundred yards (metres), turn through a gate on to open Hazely Peat Moor and continue with the wall on your right for another few hundred yards (metres). Just before you meet another wall ❸, turn down the hillside. This next section takes advantage of the new access rights, offering a relatively straightforward scramble. The objective is to pick up Hudson Quarry Lane ❹, the right of way shown on the map close to Knarlton Knot. The suggested route is down the right-hand side of Ashby Gill, where gates can be used to cross between fields.

Having reached Hudson Quarry Lane, continue northwards along the lane.

■ Close to Morpeth Scar, there are once again fine views to enjoy. Wensleydale at this point appears to split three ways, with Bishopdale and Walden to the south, the small valley of Beldon Beck to the north and Wensleydale itself continuing westwards past Aysgarth.

Bolton Castle is an obvious landmark on the opposite hillside. The castle was put up in the late fourteenth century by Richard Scrope, who was Lord Chancellor to Richard II and, later, the Archbishop of York. In 1399 Henry IV usurped the throne from Richard, but Scrope made the tactical mistake of backing the former king and Henry had him beheaded in 1405. The former archbishop was buried in his own minster in York.

Bolton Castle went on to have an eventful history which included the brief imprisonment of Mary Queen of Scots there, in 1568–9. The castle is now, deservedly, a popular visitor attraction.

▶ Continue as the lane bends round to head eastwards. Then turn left ❺ on to another track down the hill. Leave the track near woods and continue along the footpath to the remains of the Templars' chapel ❻, in a field below the woods.

■ What is now a single ruined structure was in medieval times the site, as the rather unhelpful information sign tells visitors, of a preceptory (that is, a community) of the Order of the Knights Templar.

All sorts of popular myths have become associated with

the Knights Templar over the years and the legend that they continue as a secret society dedicated to the defence of the Holy Grail provided author Dan Brown with much of the plot he needed for his best-selling *The Da Vinci Code*. Umberto Eco also went over some of

Wensleydale, near Hawes

the same entertaining material in his novel *Foucault's Pendulum*. Modern freemasonry draws heavily on Templar legends and rituals.

The old chapel in Wensleydale provides an opportunity to move beyond the myths and to encounter some of the real history of this order of soldier-monks. The Knights Templar – the Poor Knights of Christ and the Temple of Solomon – was a monastic order founded in 1118, in the aftermath of the first Crusade. The Templars initially took on the role of protecting Christian pilgrims who were visiting the Holy Land, and their name is a reference to the Temple Mount in Jerusalem.

The order started in poverty but rapidly became both wealthy (mainly through their involvement in early banking and commercial activities) and politically powerful, answerable for their activities only to the Pope. In the process they also made enemies, and in 1307 Philip, King of France, with the co-operation of Pope Clement V, seized an opportunity to have the order disbanded. On the Pope's orders, the Templars' property, as here in Wensleydale, passed to the Hospitallers (the Knights of the Hospital), another military monastic order established at the time of the Crusades.

The distinctive Knights Templar cross can be found on stones in the vicinity of the Wensleydale chapel, and you will notice one beside the gate as you approach the field containing the chapel. As the date on the stone makes clear, it was put up in the nineteenth century, shortly after the site was first excavated. Of the genuine medieval remains, the most interesting objects are the stone coffins inside the walls of the chapel.

▶ Take the footpath down to Temple Farm. The Georgian summer house directly opposite was built in the later eighteenth century by John Foss, an architect from Richmond, who also built nearby Swinithwaite Hall. Turn left and walk on the verge of the main road down the hill. Then turn right ❼ and follow Stony Stoop Lane to the stepping stones at the River Ure.

■ A number of measures have been taken in recent years to encourage otters back into the Dales rivers. For example, the Yorkshire Dales Millennium Trust has supported a project just upstream of here to make the banks of the Ure more otter-friendly. The work has included fencing off stretches of the riverside to prevent grazing by livestock.

Efforts like these seem to be paying off. Otters now appear to be present in this stretch of the Ure and are also becoming more widespread in the Swale and the lower Wharfe. It's not necessarily easy, however, to gauge exactly how well this recolonization of the rivers (which otters deserted primarily because of water pollution caused by farming) is progressing.

Otters are famously elusive and naturalists tend to calculate their numbers by monitoring the quantity of their droppings (known as spraint) to be found beside the rivers.

▶ From the stepping stones, a concessionary footpath follows the river bank for a short way, before rejoining the right of way near Middle Wood. Continue on the path until it drops down through woodland to the waterfalls at Redmire Force ❽.

■ Though the Aysgarth Falls, a little upriver, are rather more dramatic and attract more visitors, Redmire Force is nevertheless a pleasant place to pause briefly.

▶ Follow the path back uphill and continue for about ¾ mile (a little over 1 km), keeping to the field edge above the woodlands which drop down to the river. Turn right at a signpost on to another right of way, heading across fields to High Wanlass. At High Wanlass, take Flats Lane back to West Witton.

WALK 4

COVERDALE AND COLSTERDALE

DIFFICULTY

DISTANCE 11 miles (17.5 km)

| WEST SCRAFTON | THREE HOLES STOOP | COLSTERDALE | RED WAY | CALDBERGH | WEST SCRAFTON |

MAP OS Explorer OL30, Yorkshire Dales (Northern and Central) or Harveys Dales East

STARTING POINT West Scrafton (GR 073836)

PUBLIC TRANSPORT Buses currently reach Coverdale only once a week, on Fridays, to provide a service to and from the Friday market in Leyburn. Walkers using the buses will probably need to shorten slightly the walk suggested, in order to catch the last bus of the afternoon. No buses on public holidays.

PARKING This is not easy in West Scrafton. A small number of cars can be parked on the grassy verge of the road on the Caldbergh side of the village.

From one little-explored dale to another, even less well-known one. The route includes some open moorland walking in remote country. Navigation may be challenging when visibility is poor.

▶ The walk begins at Bow Bridge, in the heart of the quiet Coverdale village of West Scrafton.

■ The modern bridge is built over a much earlier stone packhorse bridge, which was indeed 'bow' arched. It's worth taking a moment to look over the bridge to the impressive limestone gorge below, carved out by the Great Gill stream.

Right under the bridge is the entrance to Scrafton Pot, a fascinating cave system which can be explored by potholers who have come prepared for the initial pitch (the vertical drop which gives access to the subterranean passages) of 65 ft (20 m).

Close by here is a cave known traditionally as Tom Hunter's Parlour. The story is that the name belongs to a highwayman who was captured in the cave.

West Scrafton was a favourite holiday destination of James Herriot (real name Alf Wight), the Yorkshire vet whose best-selling accounts of his life were made into the popular film and television series *All Creatures Great and Small*. The television programmes were filmed partly in Coverdale.

He describes in his book *James Herriot's Yorkshire* how he spent much of his holiday time in West Scrafton. He would stay in an old house beside the village green and pass his days roaming the fells with his Ordnance Survey map tucked into his anorak: 'You have only to walk out of the door and look up at the long rocky comb on the crest of Roova Crag to feel you have found somewhere exciting. The Crag overhangs the village from a height of over fifteen hundred feet and it is the pleasantest of strolls to follow the track to the summit. . . . I spent many afternoons up on the Crag with my dogs, either wandering over the mounds and tussocks or stretched out on the crisp grass.'

In fact, James Herriot may well have been trespassing. It is only since 2005 and the introduction of access legislation that public access to Great Roova has officially been permitted.

▶ The walk initially follows James Herriot's route, taking the bridleway up from West Scrafton village towards Great Roova Crags. For the energetic, it's a stiff clamber from the foot of the Crags up to the boundary fence and trig point at the top, where good views can be enjoyed back over Coverdale. Alternatively, keep to the bridleway as it swings south,

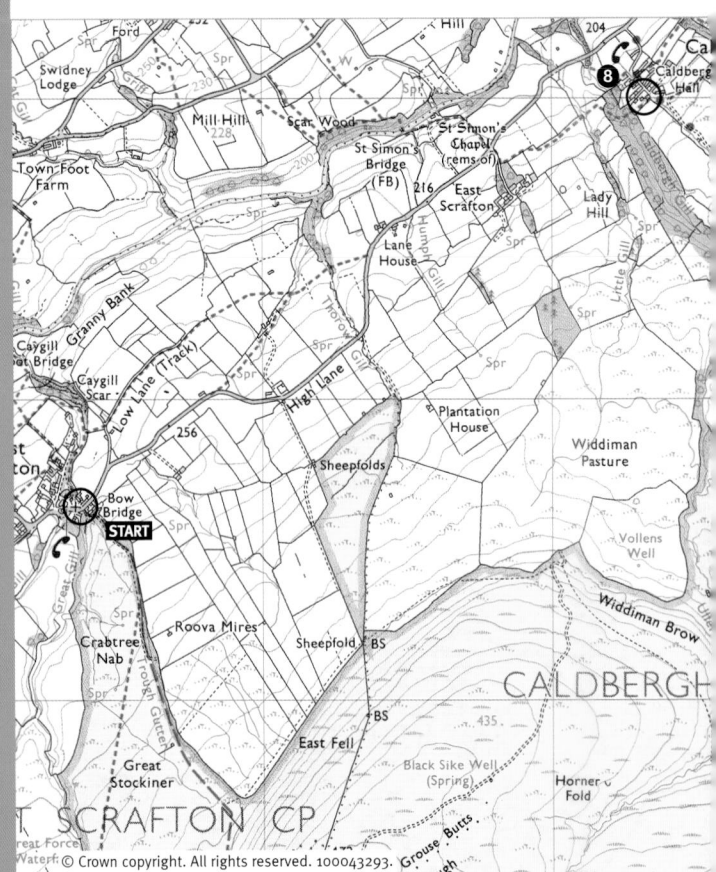

© Crown copyright. All rights reserved. 100043293.

heading up the hillside past a series of mining spoil heaps. At the hill crest, the path arrives at the fenced-in area which marks the site of West Scrafton Colliery ❶.

■ West Scrafton may be a peaceful place today, but it was once a working mining community. The colliery at West Scrafton operated until the First World War, when

▶ Map continues southwards on pages 66–7

the long tradition of exploiting the coal seams on Roova Moor finally came to an end. Coal was probably first taken from these hillsides in medieval times by the monks from nearby Jervaulx Abbey.

The mystery of two West Scrafton miners who disappeared apparently without trace in or around 1786 was only cleared up more than a century later, when their bodies were found in a closed mine. The Durham

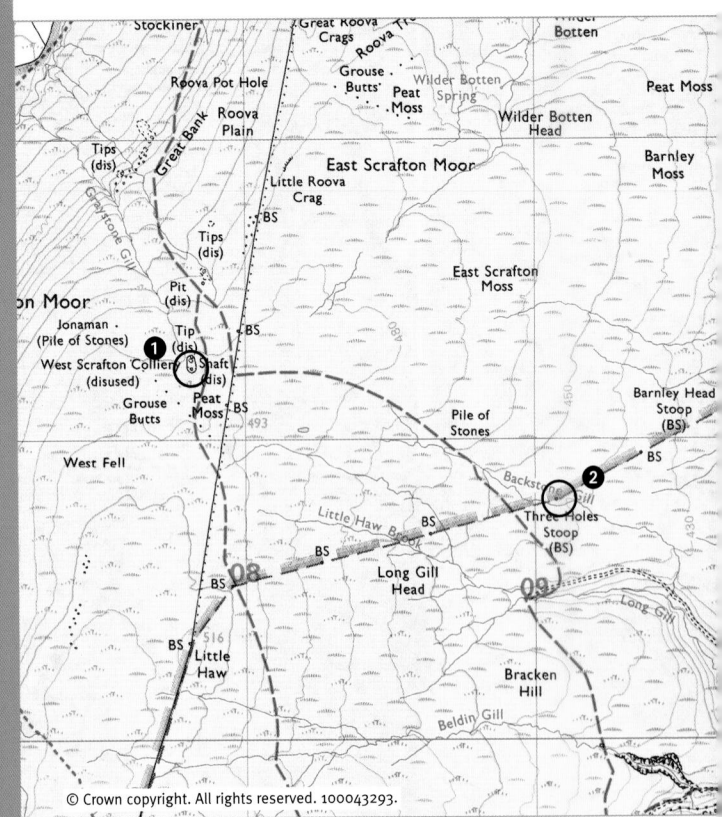

Mining Museum's online archive carries a local newspaper report from 1912 of the subsequent inquest: 'There was a tradition in the village that at the time of the West Witton fair, in August, over 120 years ago, two men had gone into the mine to bring their tools out and they never returned.' It seems likely that foul air in the mine caused the men to perish.

West Scrafton was one of a number of collieries located on the bleak, high moorland

of the Yorkshire Dales. Tan Hill (see page 119) was the most important coal-mining area in the northern Dales. Further south, another series of pits was sunk on the exposed flank of Fountains Fell, near Malham.

▶ At the colliery remains, turn left on to a path which heads eastwards to a nearby gate in the boundary fence. Cross the stile here and continue over the isolated moors. Although this route is officially a bridleway, there is barely a trace of path on the ground to follow. A series of wooden stakes point (broadly) the right direction.

■ Shortly after crossing boggy Backstone Gill, look out for the boundary stone a short distance away to the left, beside the stream. This is Three Holes Stoop (stoop being the northern term for a guide stone or boundary stone) ❷.

The stone is beautifully carved with the words 'Mashamshire, 3 holes, 5 yards S.W.'. The inscription refers to the line of the historic administrative boundary a short distance away, though the reference to 'three holes' is less immediately easy to explain.

Three Holes Stoop is one of a number of boundary stones which can be found, often almost hidden, on the moors. Although the wild wastes here might seem of little value, the boundary between the different landholdings has historically been bitterly contested. In the sixteenth century, a dispute cropped up between two neighbouring landowners, Sir Christopher Danby and the Earl of Derby, over the right to stalk deer on these moors.

A few years later, in 1607, there was another legal dispute, between the Danby estate and Edward, Lord Bruce of East Witton. More than a century and a half later, the boundary between Masham and East Witton was yet again disputed and subject to legal arbitration.

The invisible border demarcated by Three Holes

Stoop and the other boundary stones on Caldbergh Moor remains important today, as the division between the local authority areas of Richmondshire and Harrogate. The stone also marks the edge of the Yorkshire Dales National Park. Beyond here, we leave the national park and enter what has been designated as the Nidderdale Area of Outstanding Natural Beauty.

▶ Drop down through the heather heading roughly south, to find the shooting track above Long Gill. Although the bridleway continues on the other side of the valley, most walkers will choose at this point to opt for some easier walking and follow the track down the valley, heading first east and then south-east.

At the bottom, the track fords both Long Gill and then, almost immediately, the main stream forming the infant River Burn ❸. When water levels are high, both fords may involve getting walking boots wet.

Keep to the south side of the river, on the track, until you reach a shooting lodge. Here it's worth dropping back down to the river to cross it by the little 'millennium bridge' that has recently been constructed ❹. Continue beside the river, this time with the water on your right, until the moor ends and pastures begin.

■ The valley which gradually opens up beyond this point is Colsterdale, a beautiful quiet valley on the edge of the Dales. The River Burn flows on eastwards into lower Wensleydale, joining the Ure just south of Masham.

Colsterdale has been important as a centre of coal mining both in medieval and more recent times. In 1334, a legal agreement between Jervaulx Abbey and Sir Geffrey le Scrop gave the monks the right to take coal from the land here. In exchange the abbey agreed 'to be bound in eight marks sterling of yearly rent, to be paid to the said Sir Geffrey and to his heirs'.

Colsterdale is also remembered for its role in the early months of the First World War, when the First Leeds Battalion (the Leeds 'Pals') were accommodated in a hastily created training camp in the area. The camp was located 1 mile (1.6 km) or so lower down the dale near Breary Banks, on land which Leeds Corporation had already acquired as part of the city's plans to create the new Leighton reservoir.

▶ At the moor end wall turn up the hillside, following the edge of the moor. Turn right with the wall, scrambling down the steep side of House Gill and back up the other side. Again turn left, to follow the wall at the moor edge, before leaving it ❺ to head back out over the open moor towards the isolated trig point ❻. If visibility is poor, use a compass at this point, aiming just east of due north.

Continue roughly due north beyond the trig point. After about six or seven minutes' further walking (approximately 500 yards/500 m), you will meet an old, deeply sunken hollow way, running up from Colsterdale. Turn left on to the track, and follow it as it leads back westwards, high up above the side of Birk Gill.

■ As can be easily deduced from the way the track has sunk into the moor, this is an old route which has long been used by travellers between Colsterdale and Coverdale. As the map reveals, however, only the section closest to Coverdale, in what is now the Richmondshire local authority area, has been recorded as a right of way. On the Colsterdale side of the boundary, no right of way was entered when the 'definitive map' for the parish was first drawn up.

It is surprisingly common in upland country to find rights of way which appear to stop abruptly on reaching a parish boundary. The National Parks and Access to the Countryside Act 1949 required local authorities to produce definitive maps marking public rights of way, but some authorities were more thorough than others. In some areas, too, landowners (particularly those with grouse moors) were not unhappy when old routes failed to make it on to the maps.

Even though there are now legal rights of access to open moorland, it is still important that historic public routes are properly designated as rights of way. In addition to introducing access legislation, the Countryside and Rights of Way Act 2000 has also established a cut-off date of 2026 after which it will no longer be possible for traditional footpaths, bridleways and tracks to be added to definitive maps. The Ramblers' Association is encouraging its members to look for documentary evidence of old rights of way, in order to ensure that they become designated before the 2026 deadline is reached.

▶ Continue along the old track, splashing through (or leaping over) the ford marked as Slip Wath. At the hill crest ❼, the valley of Coverdale abruptly opens up below.

From the hill brow, it's possible to make your way across country back to Great Roova Crags. The suggested route continues north, however, following the Red Way down to Caldbergh village. Pen Hill (Walk 3) and Harland Hill come into sight beyond.

■ As the Red Way drops down the hillside, an earlier hollow way can be seen a little to the left. Parallel hollow ways like these are usually a good indication of an historical packhorse route: when the first hollow way became muddy or hard to use, the packhorse teams would begin to start a new line across the hillside.

▶ At Caldbergh ❽, take the pleasant field footpath signposted to East Scrafton. Follow the road briefly to Lane House and then take field paths to Low Lane, returning to West Scrafton.

Who should live in the Dales?

It's a beautiful area, and visitors to the national park often envy those who can call the Yorkshire Dales their home. In fact, it can be a pleasant fantasy if you're in the Dales on holiday to check out the house prices in the local estate agents' windows and to engage in a little 'what if?' dreaming.

Every year some people go beyond the dreaming stage, however, and actually buy their own property in the Dales. For these lucky ones, it's the start of an absorbing time getting to know the area and its history better. But house buying by people who live outside the area also raises some quite tricky social questions which the national park authority has recently been trying to tackle.

Roughly 20,000 people live within the boundaries of the national park, and to accommodate them there are just over 10,000 houses available. Of this total housing stock, however, about 15 per cent is in use either as second homes for people with their main homes elsewhere or as holiday homes available for letting. In some parts of the Dales, the percentage of holiday homes is much higher, in some villages even rising to as high as two houses in every three.

Visitors who come to stay in these houses bring money into the local economy and help the many tourist attractions keep going. But there can be less satisfactory outcomes too. For example, if fewer people are living week-in week-out in the Dales it can be more difficult for local shops and pubs to survive or for adequate public transport to be provided. The whole infrastructure of local social and cultural life, everything which keeps a community living and thriving, can begin to be in jeopardy.

In the heart of the Yorkshire Dales

The inflation of house prices by outside pressures creates a particular problem for local young people when they reach the stage of wanting to set up their own homes. It's certainly true that the Dales is an expensive place to buy property: on average, houses are approaching double the national average and are certainly far more pricey than houses elsewhere in the Yorkshire region. A further complication is that many former council houses are no longer available for renting. In the years between 1991 and 2001, 241 council house tenants in the Dales exercised their 'right to buy', transferring these houses from the social housing sector on to the open market.

As the national park authority has pointed out, high house prices in the Dales are coupled with low average incomes, since more than one in three of the working population earn their living in agriculture.

All in all, it's not surprising that Census figures show that the Dales area has more older people and fewer children than the national average. And this has further implications: if pupil numbers continue to fall, the future of village schools, another key feature of the life of many communities, can become threatened.

So what can be done? In recent years the Yorkshire Dales National Park Authority has come up with an innovative idea which, it believes, may help. It proposes that future sales of new homes within the Dales area will be restricted, to meet only 'local needs'. The exact way that local needs are to be defined is complex, but groups that will be eligible for the new houses include existing residents within the national park who are establishing their own homes, people who are moving to take up existing jobs in the Dales and past residents of the area who still have family living locally and who want to move back.

The need for a policy such as this, not just in the Yorkshire Dales but also in other rural areas, was backed up by a report published in late 2004 by the housing charity Shelter, which pointed out that the number of second homes in Britain was increasing dramatically, by around 15 per cent a year. 'Rural life as we know it is under threat,' Shelter claimed. 'There is a real danger that living in the countryside will become the preserve of the wealthy.'

Nevertheless, not everyone has been in favour of the new strategy. Some local estate agents, for example, argued strongly that the overall needs of both house buyers and sellers are best met by the workings of the open market. Start imposing restrictions on the market, they said, and things could quickly start going awry.

Despite these caveats, early in 2005 the national park authority decided to press ahead, taking an in-principle decision to make the change. The media quickly picked up on what they realized was an important story. 'New Dales homes: only locals need apply' read one national newspaper headline at the time.

With all this publicity, it is perhaps easy to exaggerate exactly what has been discussed and agreed. When the policy of 'local homes for local people' is in force, it will apply only to new houses built within the Park area – probably a total of no more than around 700 over the next few years. Nobody is suggesting that the 10,000 or so existing houses in the Dales should be made subject to these restrictions; it would surely be legally impossible to try to do so. The vast majority of houses, therefore, will continue to be sold on the open market, at whatever prices the buyers and sellers want to agree.

This means that local authorities, and local people, will have to continue to try to tackle the issues created by the presence of holiday homes in the national park. It also means, though, that visitors to the Yorkshire Dales will have nothing to stop them from dreaming.

WALK 5

MAIDEN CASTLE AND HARKER HILL

DIFFICULTY 👢 👢 **DISTANCE 5¾ miles (9.5 km)**

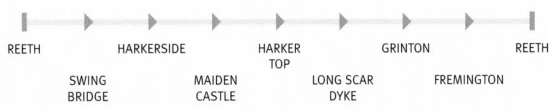

REETH — HARKERSIDE — HARKER TOP — GRINTON — REETH

SWING BRIDGE — MAIDEN CASTLE — LONG SCAR DYKE — FREMINGTON

MAP OS Explorer OL30, Yorkshire Dales (Northern and Central) or Harveys Dales North

STARTING POINT Reeth (GR 038992)

PUBLIC TRANSPORT Buses run from Richmond. There are also services from Darlington/Hawes on summer Sundays/Bank Holidays, and from Leeds/Wakefield on some summer Sundays.

PARKING In the centre of Reeth

Relatively straightforward walking, primarily on tracks and footpaths, though with a stiff climb to High Harker Hill. This walk includes the chance to explore the hill fort of Maiden Castle and other early earthworks.

■ Today Reeth is Swaledale's main centre of tourism, and its attractive green is busy with visitors in summer months. Historically, however, Reeth's wealth came from industry, in particular from the lead mining which dominated Swaledale for many centuries. Reeth was also the focus for another important economic activity, the knitting industry.

The walk begins beside Hudson House, the information and enterprise centre at one corner of the green. This building was previously a branch of Barclays Bank. Barclays' decision in 2000 to close the branch, effectively leaving the upper Swale valley without banking facilities, was controversial and hard fought at the time by local people.

▶ Take the lane beyond Hudson House and follow the sign 'To the river'. Continue, turning left when in doubt, to find the footpath signed to the Swing Bridge. Carry on until you reach the banks of the Swale.

■ Reeth's Swing Bridge ❶ is, of course, no such thing, but rather a suspension bridge – though it is true that it can swing a little when several people are crossing at the same time.

The current bridge replaces an earlier one, which (as a small display board recounts) was swept away in September 2000 when the river was in spate. The present bridge copies the design of the original.

▶ Beyond the bridge, the footpath up the hill to Harkerside Place Farm is well signed. Pass the farm buildings, to reach the minor road from Grinton. Turn right. Almost immediately, as soon as you reach open ground, turn left and cross the heather aiming for the prominent barrow ahead.

■ This tumulus is the first of several prehistoric sites visited on the walk. The main objective at this point, however, lies just beyond here. What looks initially like a walled lane is in fact the impressive entrance to Maiden Castle ❷, an old 'hill fort'.

The entrance corridor to Maiden Castle is more than 100 yards (100 m) long and 10 ft (3 m) and more in width. It gives the whole complex what has been called its 'banjo' shape (a term which

▶ page 80

becomes particularly apposite when the site is seen in aerial photographs). In this respect Maiden Castle differs from the Yorkshire Dales' best-known hill fort, on Ingleborough hill a little way off to the south-west. Other banjo hill enclosures are found elsewhere in Britain, primarily in southern counties, though these tend to be smaller in size.

Maiden Castle itself is a large open expanse of ground surrounded on all sides by substantial earthworks. It is generally assumed to be later prehistoric (in other words, Iron Age), perhaps dating back to 600 BC. Some consider it may be later, dating from the Romano-British period. On the other hand, the nearby barrows are likely to be considerably older, dating back to the early Bronze Age or even the late neolithic period.

Although it is convenient shorthand to describe Maiden Castle as a hill fort, this may not be strictly correct. As many people

have pointed out, it is not particularly well located for defence purposes. Whatever its primary function, however, it is an impressive human creation, 'a prehistoric monument of national importance,' according to Mark Bowden and Keith Blood, two archaeologists

who have recently undertaken a reassessment of the site.

Not the least of Maiden Castle's attractions is the fine view over the Swale valley below.

▶ After exploring Maiden Castle, clamber up the hillside to the south and head off across the heather. Very shortly, you will find a footpath (shown on OS maps). Turn left, and follow the path briefly eastwards, before turning back to the right to pick up the path running diagonally up the hillside. The path climbs steadily up the side of High Harker Hill. Beyond a row of grouse butts, turn right beside

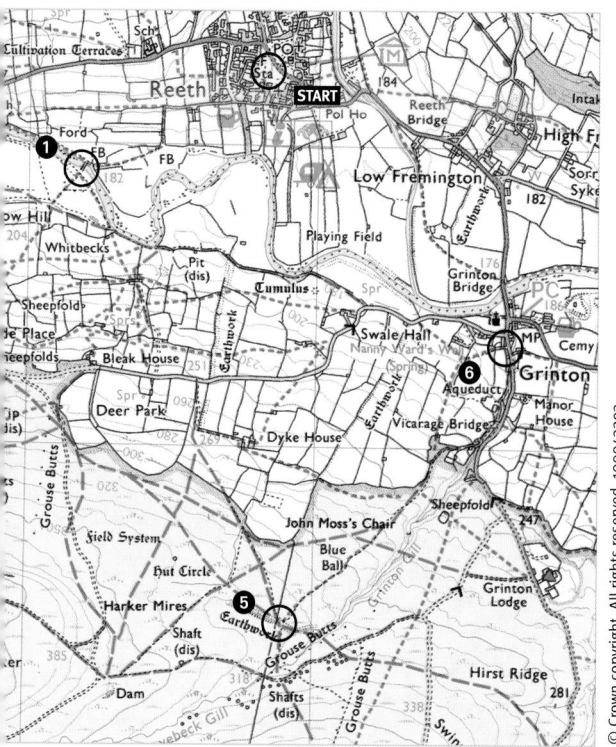

a drainage ditch to emerge on
to the summit ❸.

■ Like Maiden Castle below,
the ground at Harker Top is a
mass of earthworks, mounds
and ditches, but this is the
result of more recent human
history. The Harkerside
moorland can today seem
isolated, but for centuries
it was an important area of
lead mining.

The history of mining here
can be traced back to
at least 1628 when a local
landowner, Humphrey
Wharton, acquired a twenty-
one-year lease to the mines
on Harkerside, as well
as those in Grinton and
Fremington. Almost certainly,
however, lead mining had
already been taking place
at the time when the lease
was acquired.

Swaledale has seen lead
mining since medieval times.
A royal mandate of 1215
made reference to the miners
of Swaledale, and a lead
mine is known to have been
operating in Arkengarthdale
in the late thirteenth century.

The right to license lead
mining was a valuable asset
for landowners, and as such
could be the cause of legal
disputes. The mining rights
on Harkerside were the
subject of prolonged legal
action in the eighteenth
century, in which once
again the Wharton family
were involved.

▶ Turn left on the shooting track.

■ As the track begins to
descend from the Harker
Top plateau it crosses the
impressive earthwork known
as Long Scar Dyke ❹. The
dyke is a significant work
of engineering, once again
perhaps dating back to Iron
Age times. It extends for
about ⅔ mile (1 km) south-
westwards, making use of the
natural brow of Harker Top.

Long Scar Dyke is one of a
series of similar earthworks
and dykes in this part of
upper Swaledale (another
earthwork, Harker Mires
Dyke, will be passed shortly).
The conventional explanation
is that they date back to Iron

Age times, before the Roman occupation of Britain. This was certainly the opinion of the distinguished Yorkshire historian Arthur Raistrick.

More recently, however, another theory has been put forward, suggesting that the dykes were erected in post-Roman times to mark the boundary between British (in other words, Celtic) and Anglian kingdoms, the latter situated further down the Swale valley.

Whatever the origin of these earthworks, it certainly seems that there was a time in post-Roman Britain when this area of Yorkshire was on the front line between Anglian and British areas of settlement. Intriguingly, the *Gododdin*, attributed to the celebrated Welsh bard Aneirin and one of the oldest surviving poems in Old Welsh, tells the epic tale of a battle between a united army of Celtic warriors and their Anglian opponents, which seems to have taken place close to the River Swale around AD 590–600. In the poem the battle is located at Catraeth, which has been identified by Kenneth Jackson in his English translation of the *Gododdin* as modern-day Catterick.

Although the *Gododdin* was created in the language which has developed into modern Welsh, it is in a sense actually a Scottish poem, since the Gododdin were a Celtic-speaking people living in the lands around what today is Edinburgh. The warriors from Gododdin allied themselves with other armies, including a party from north Wales, to tackle their Anglian enemies. But the venture turned out disastrously, and only the poet and one of the warriors (some versions say three) came back alive from Catraeth.

Nevertheless, the poem strikes a heroic note: 'Three hundred men hastened forth, wearing gold torques, defending the land – and there was slaughter. Though they were slain they slew, and they shall be honoured till the end of the world . . .'

▶ Carry on down the hill, at the bottom continuing straight ahead on to a more grassy track over the moorland. Pass through a gate in a boundary fence and immediately turn left, crossing Grovebeck Gill and making for the earthwork known as Harker Mires Dyke ❺.

Continue through another gate and take the well-defined track heading north-eastwards towards Grinton village. As you leave open country behind, take the footpath past a barn and across fields just to the west of Grinton village. Turn right, on to the field path which emerges close to Grinton church ❻.

■ St Andrew's in Grinton was for many centuries the only parish church serving upper Swaledale. This meant that the bodies of those who died further up the valley had to be carried down to Grinton for burial.

An old 'corpse way' became established, from Keld over Kisdon Hill to Muker and then across the Swale at the Ramps Holme ford. It followed the north bank of the river – the sunny side of the valley. The corpse would be carried in a coffin made of wicker and the journey often took two days, with the coffin bearers staying overnight near Gunnerside.

The tradition of carrying bodies from the upper Swaledale villages to Grinton came to an end after a chapel and consecrated burial ground were opened in Muker in the sixteenth century. However, Muker remained a daughter church of Grinton for three centuries more, only becoming a parish in its own right in 1892.

Between the church and the river is the beautiful old house known as Blackburn Hall. Its name comes from the family who owned it during the eighteenth century. The house carries a datestone from 1635.

▶ Cross the bridge and immediately take a field footpath left, through the water meadows.

■ To the right of the footpath, just before you reach the road at Fremington, is an old water mill, with the water wheel still in place. The leat (channel) which carried water from the Arkle Beck to the wheel is also easy to spot, although now dry and overgrown.

▶ Walk back along the main road into Reeth.

Cattle in pastureland, Swaledale

Swaledale sheep

Sheep farmers know that, for many visitors to the countryside, a sheep is simply a sheep – a white woolly creature that bleats, hangs around in a flock, grazes away at the grass and periodically gets itself stuck on a ledge or in a bog.

But for farmers the idea of being unable to distinguish, say, a Swaledale sheep from a Wensleydale sheep is as unthinkable as being unable to tell a terrier from a labrador. Like dogs, sheep have been bred by humans over the centuries to meet particular needs. Different sheep breeds (and the UK's National Sheep Association records over eighty, from Badger Face Welsh Mountain and Beltex to Wiltshire Horn and Zwartble) are suitable for different terrains, and what is ideal for the gentle lowland pasturelands of the south won't do very well on the rough fells of northern England.

Swaledales have been bred for the tough life. Even for those of us who are not farmers they're one of the easier breeds of sheep to recognize, with fine curly horns and attractive dark and light ('black' and 'white') markings on their faces. Helpfully for visitors to the Yorkshire Dales, the Swaledale sheep has provided the model for the familiar national park logo.

Swaledales emerged as a distinct breed over a period of some time. Their antecedents were a horned type, from which other breeds such as the Blackface and Rough Fell also developed. By the early twentieth century the breed had become well established and just after the First World War a group of farmers living close to Tan Hill decided it was time to create what would become the Swaledale Sheep Breeders Association.

Along with the creation of the Breeders Association went the establishment, in 1920, of the flock book, the central register which records the bloodlines of Swaledale pure-breds. As with other pedigree animals, the best sheep are generally those which come from the best stock and, particularly for pedigree rams, some really significant sums of money can be involved. The very highest price yet paid at auction for a ram (or 'tup') was an astonishing £101,000. While that price is exceptional, each year the best animals will normally command at least £20,000–£35,000. Tups with this sort of price on their head are, needless to say, expected to earn their keep in the way nature intended when the tupping season comes round each November. Incidentally, the Swaledale Sheep Breeders Association has recently moved to ban artificial insemination for pedigree sheep, as a way of continuing to ensure a sufficiently broad genetic pool for the breed.

Swaledales are valued highly because they are one of the premier breeds – indeed, some would say *the* premier breed – of hill sheep. As the Breeders Association puts it, the Swaledale is 'a bold, hardy sheep, well fitted to endure the hardships of exposed and high-lying situations'. As well as being content with the limited diet that comes their way, the ewes also have a reputation for good motherhood. Provided they are well managed, they breed prolifically and are good at producing milk and looking after their lambs.

Even better, when pure-bred Swaledale ewes are bred with Bluefaced Leicester rams, the result is an extremely popular and commercial crossbreed known, logically enough, as a Mule. Mules are fast growing, easy to shepherd and also breed prolifically. For many farmers of Swaledale sheep, therefore, the key to success is access to a good stock of Bluefaced Leicester tups, to keep a supply of Mules coming each spring. Some farmers, however, are trying other breeding combinations, in recent years crossing their Swaledale ewes with tups from Texel and Beltex breeds.

Swaledale sheep, bred for the tough life

Agriculture in the Dales is primarily livestock farming, with the focus on sheep and beef cattle. (There are also some dairy herds in lower Dales areas.) For sheep farmers, the yearly cycle of work could be said to start with tupping time in November. Lambs are born the following April, which not surprisingly is the busiest month of the year. May typically sees the ewes and lambs moved on to higher pastures, together with any hoggs which are being kept in the flock (hogg is the name used for the previous year's lambs, now at the intermediate stage between lambs and fully adult breeding sheep). Silage is cut and baled for winter use in June, and this task is followed by the shearing of the ewes and, for the first time, of the hoggs.

Autumn is the main season for sheep auctions, with local marts held in Hawes, Kirkby Stephen and Middleton-in-Teesdale. There is a sequence to these sales, too, with Mule ewes tending to come to market first and pedigree Swaledale rams last of all. Kirkby Stephen mart, to take one example, probably sees something like a thousand Swaledale rams and 20,000 ewes pass through its hands each year – and these figures relate to the breeding animals, not those sheep destined for the butchery trade.

Swaledale sheep can now be found far away from Yorkshire, but they still remain a familiar sight on the fells surrounding the dale which gave them their name. Curiously, it is in the Swaledale area itself that farmers tend to have their own way of pronouncing the breed: not so much a two-syllabic 'swale-dale', more an abbreviated 'swardle'.

WALK 6

KISDON, SWINNER GILL AND GUNNERSIDE

DIFFICULTY 👟 👟 👟   **DISTANCE 11 miles (17.5 km)**

MUKER — KISDON HILL — EAST STONESDALE BRIDGE — SWINNER GILL — LOWNATH-WAITE — GUNNERSIDE — CALVERT HOUSES — MUKER

MAP OS Explorer OL30, Yorkshire Dales (Northern and Central) or Harveys Dales North

STARTING POINT Muker (GR 911978)

PUBLIC TRANSPORT Buses run from Richmond. There are also services from Darlington/Hawes on summer Sundays/Bank Holidays, and from Leeds/Wakefield on some summer Sundays.

PARKING Pay-and-display car park in Muker

Of all the walks in this book, this is the one which visits areas most closely associated with the lead-mining industry. But that should not deter: this is still a beautiful walk, through some of the most attractive Dales landscapes. The walking is on tracks and footpaths throughout (with the option of some open-country walking).

■ There are several paths to choose from when walking between Muker and Keld, including a low-level path which follows the River Swale upstream. The suggested route, however, opts for some initial climbing, in order to pick up the path over Kisdon Hill which is also followed by the Pennine Way. Alfred Wainwright described the route as 'a magnificent terrace high above the Swale', adding, 'If only the whole of the Pennine Way were as pleasant as this!' (Wainwright was never particularly keen on the wilder and peatier sections of the Pennine Way.)

▶ Passing the church, take Muker's main street up from the B6270 Reeth road. Keep to the left of the post office, following the lane past the former Muker vicarage. Continue along the rough road up the hillside towards the farm at Kisdon. When you reach the first house at Kisdon ❶, turn right picking up the Pennine Way. Continue for almost 2 miles (3 km), enjoying the fine views down to the Swale river far below. Ahead, across the Swale, the Swinner Gill valley can be seen.

■ As the path begins to approach Keld, a footpath off to the right marks the way down to Kisdon Force waterfall on the Swale. Even if the idea of an optional diversion downhill doesn't appeal, you will certainly hear the noise from Kisdon Force at this point.

▶ The Pennine Way finally drops down to the Swale at the East Stonesdale bridge ❷ (as mentioned on page 108, this very attractive spot is the place where the Pennine Way and the Coast to Coast path cross). Once over the bridge, turn right to take the track along the north side of the Swale. There's a good view down to the top of Kisdon Force. Continue to the ruined houses at Crackpot Hall ❸.

■ The hillside behind Crackpot Hall, from East Stonesdale across to Swinner Gill, was an area of extensive lead mining. The mines at Beldi Hill were the setting for a complex legal dispute which took place in the late 1760s and early 1770s. The

▶ page 94

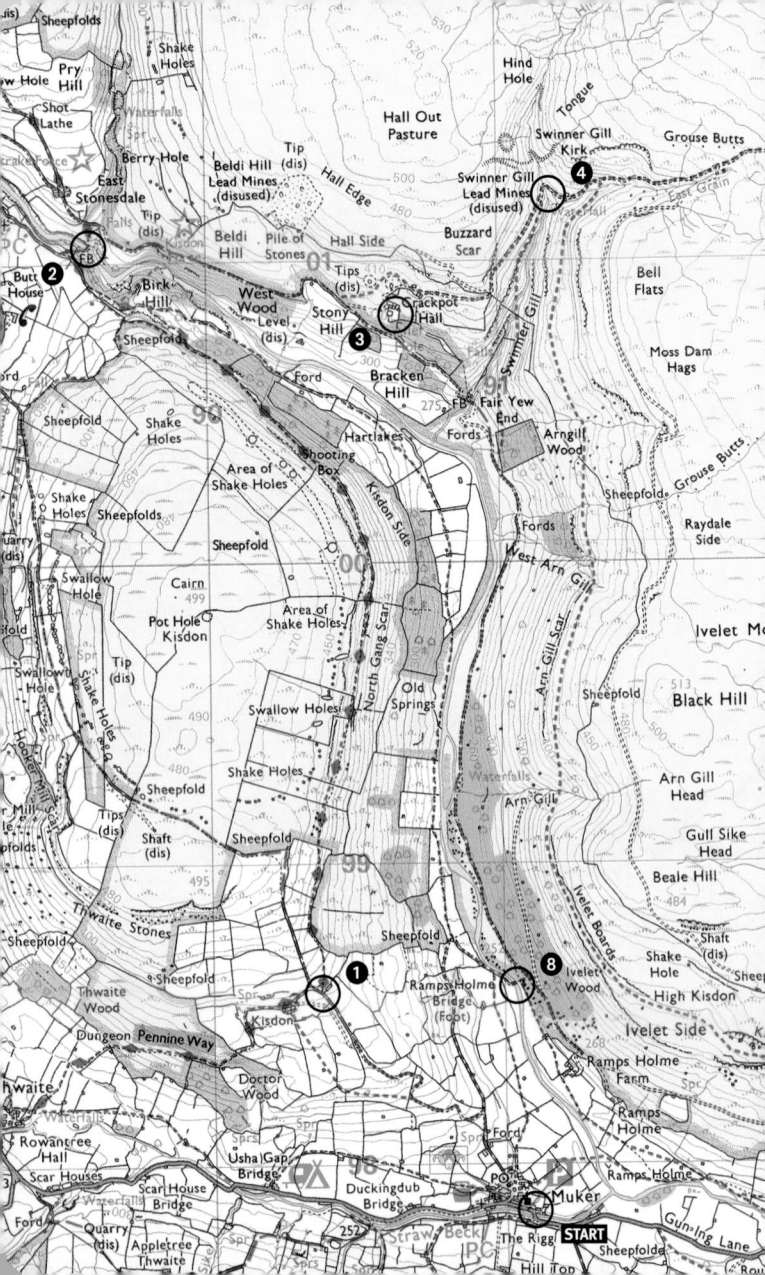

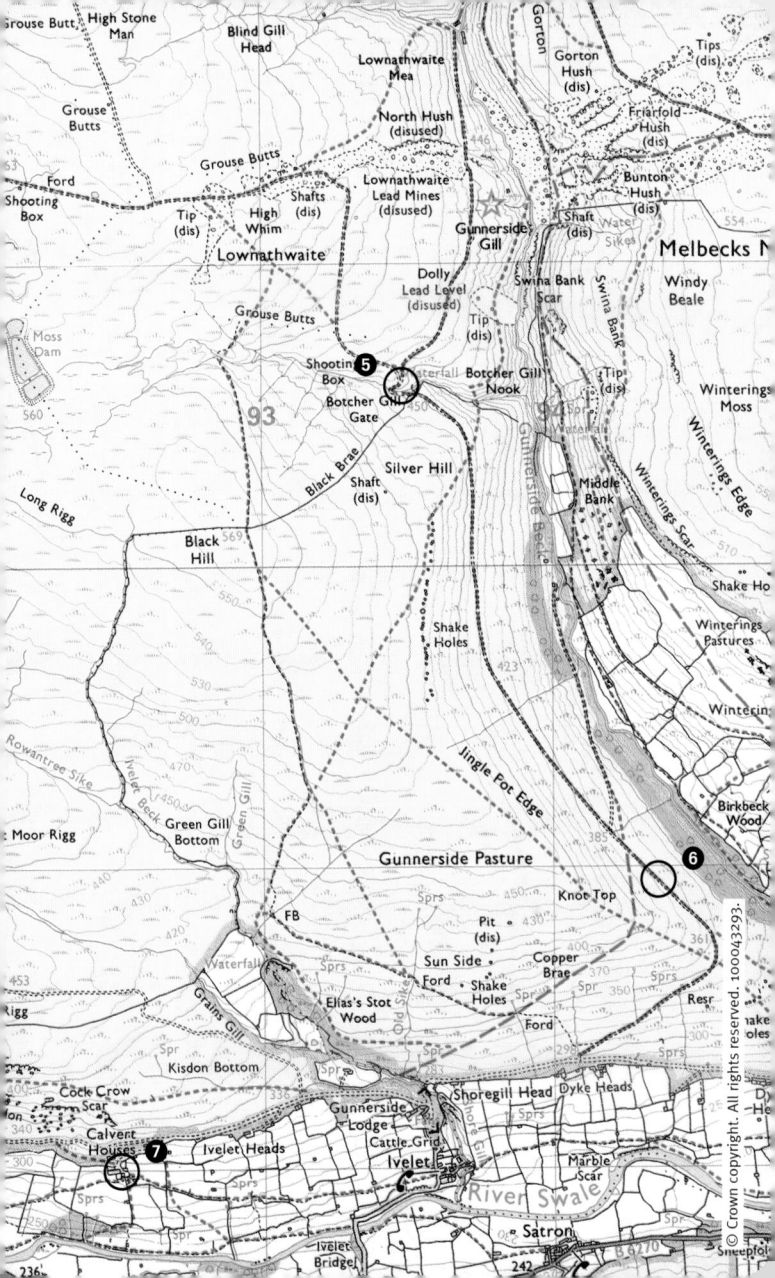

case hinged on whether a key mining concession near Crackpot Hall was part of the manor of Muker – and therefore on whether the lord of the manor, Lord Pomfret, was entitled to royalties on the rich vein of lead being mined there. Lord Pomfret took the case all the way to the House of Lords, where, eventually, judgment went against him. Impoverished by the court actions, he was imprisoned for debt.

While the dispute was raging in the courts, the miners on each side took matters into their own hands, attempting to sabotage the other side's mining operations, for example by diverting streams down mine shafts.

Crackpot Hall was reputedly built originally as a hunting lodge. The ruins have recently been awarded grant funding to prevent further dereliction. The story of the house is given on a small plaque at the entrance, which also offers an explanation for the unusual name, suggesting that it comes from the Norse for a pot or chasm frequented by crows.

▶ Follow the track behind Crackpot Hall, past the ruined house above, continuing as it bends around the side of Swinner Gill.

■ Down beside the waters of Swinner Gill, almost due east of Crackpot Hall, was the entrance to the Parkes Level, a tunnel which extended into the hill for more than 400 yards (400 m). Built between 1647 and 1649, the Parkes Level was one of many similar levels or adits which were burrowed into the hillside in the mining areas of Beldi Hill, Swinner Gill and Gunnerside.

The stone-faced openings to levels remain in many former lead-mining areas. The site of Parkes Level cannot be seen from the track from Crackpot Hall, but another example is very visible, just below the bridge over Swinner Gill. This was Swinner Gill Main Level, which was driven northwards into the hillside. Near by are the ruins of a former smelt mill and a dressing floor (see page 20).

▶ After crossing the Swinner Gill bridge ❹, follow the path up the left bank of East Grain. Near the top, the path meets a shooting track. Turn left, and follow the track over the hill.

Keep on the shooting track as it bends round to the south above Gunnerside Beck. (A footpath leaves to the left, which can be followed northwards beyond Lownathwaite Mea to the Blakethwaite coal mines at the head of the valley.) Remain on the track, to reach the gate in the fence very close to a waterfall on Botcher Gill ❺.

■ Gunnerside Beck was a particularly important lead-mining area, where the east–west veins which were also mined from Beldi Hill and Swinner Gill were exploited. The devastated landscape on the opposite hillside is the result of hushings. Several major hushes, including Bunton Hush, Friarfold Hush and Gorton Hush, scoured out the topsoil to expose the underlying rock.

One of the most ambitious engineering feats, the Sir Francis Level, was pushed through in the mid-nineteenth century to reach the rich lead veins between Gunnerside and Old Gang, a little way to the east. The level began 1 mile (1.6 km) or so to the south, on the west bank of Gunnerside Gill (GR 940000).

The work began in 1864, and was hard going. In his account of the Wensleydale and Swaledale lead industry, historian Arthur Raistick reports that it took five years to cut the first 202 fathoms (a fathom being 6 ft or approximately 1.9 metres), at a cost of £10 a fathom. Thereafter work progressed faster, but still took almost another decade. The Sir Francis was eventually completed, at a total distance of over 500 fathoms, in the late 1870s. It was given an official opening with brass

▶ page 98

Kisdon Force, near Keld

bands in attendance, and a hydraulic pumping engine was installed deep inside the level. However, the Sir Francis was finished and ready for work just as the lead industry in Swaledale was entering the final years of its long history.

To find the opening to the Sir Francis Level, now partially flooded, drop down the hill from the shooting track ⅓ mile (0.5 km) or so after passing Botcher Gill Gate. It's a stiff climb down, and of course an even stiffer climb back up. The metal cylinder above the level opening was an air receiver for the hydraulic engine. Just downstream are the remains of two crushing mills and dressing floors.

▶ The shooting track can be followed down to the minor road from Gunnerside village near Dyke Heads. (Alternatively, near Knot Top ❻, take the opportunity to head up over open country, aiming for the road close to Shoregill Head. The bridleway shown on the map is not there on the ground, but you can take sheep trods for some of the way.)

Follow the minor road past Gunnerside Lodge to Calvert Houses ❼. Here find the field footpath which runs westwards down to the Swale.

■ The map shows this right of way crossing the Swale by a ford at Ramps Holme water meadow. This is an ancient ford, probably used as part of the 'corpse way' when bodies were carried from upper Swaledale to the churchyard at Grinton (see page 84). But these days fording the Swale here is frequently a considerable challenge – or frankly impossible. The suggested route therefore is the safe one: continue beside the river, to cross by the Ramps Holme bridge slightly further upstream.

▶ Cross the bridge ❽ and return to Muker by the field footpath.

WALK 7

LOVELY SEAT AND GREAT SHUNNER FELL

DIFFICULTY 👟 👟 👟 👟 👟

DISTANCE 11 miles (17.5 km)

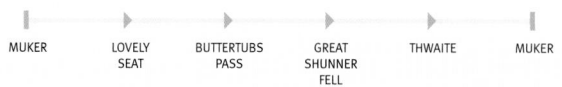

| MUKER | LOVELY SEAT | BUTTERTUBS PASS | GREAT SHUNNER FELL | THWAITE | MUKER |

MAP OS Explorer OL30, Yorkshire Dales (Northern and Central) or Harveys Dales North

STARTING POINT Muker (GR 911978)

PUBLIC TRANSPORT Buses run from Richmond. There are services from Darlington/Hawes on summer Sundays/Bank Holidays, and from Leeds/Wakefield on some summer Sundays.

PARKING Pay-and-display car park in Muker

This is a walk for those who love the wild empty moors and who are confident in navigating their way across rough open ground, using map and compass. Choose a day with good visibility, not least to benefit from the fine views.

■ Muker's old Literary Institute, set up above the main road close to the village hall and church, is a prominent architectural feature of this attractive Swaledale village. Muker was one of about fifty Dales towns and villages which erected their own literary institutes or reading rooms in Victorian times. There were similar buildings in, for example, Thwaite, Keld, Askrigg, Wham and Thornton Rust, as well as in larger communities such as Hawes and Bainbridge. In many cases, the buildings remain today.

The aim was self-improvement, although there was also a strong element of middle-class paternalism involved. At Keld, for example, the Reverend James Wilkinson was the driving force behind the establishment of a literary institute in 1862. 'How can we expect young men to avoid places of evil resort, unless more suitable places be provided for them?' he asked rhetorically. The answer, he felt, was to create a comfortable place for them to go, well equipped with 'a good supply of interesting and instructive books'.

Muker's literary institute is now used for the rehearsals of the Muker Silver Band, another Victorian initiative (it was founded in 1897) still going strong today. One of the few remaining brass bands in the northern Yorkshire Dales, it is proud of the fact that the great majority of its players come from Muker itself or from the area immediately around the village.

▶ Leave Muker, taking the bridleway (Occupation Road) on the south side of the river, beside the main car park. Follow this old lane up the side of the hill, enjoying fine views down to the village and to Kisdon Hill beyond.

The track levels out as it is joined by another lane from the left. Just before the track crosses Greenseat Beck and before another bridleway joins from the right, turn left through a field gate ❶. A grassy track heads up the hillside, rapidly swinging round so that an old stone wall is directly to the left.

Follow the track to Greenseat Gate ❷, where you reach the

▶ page 104

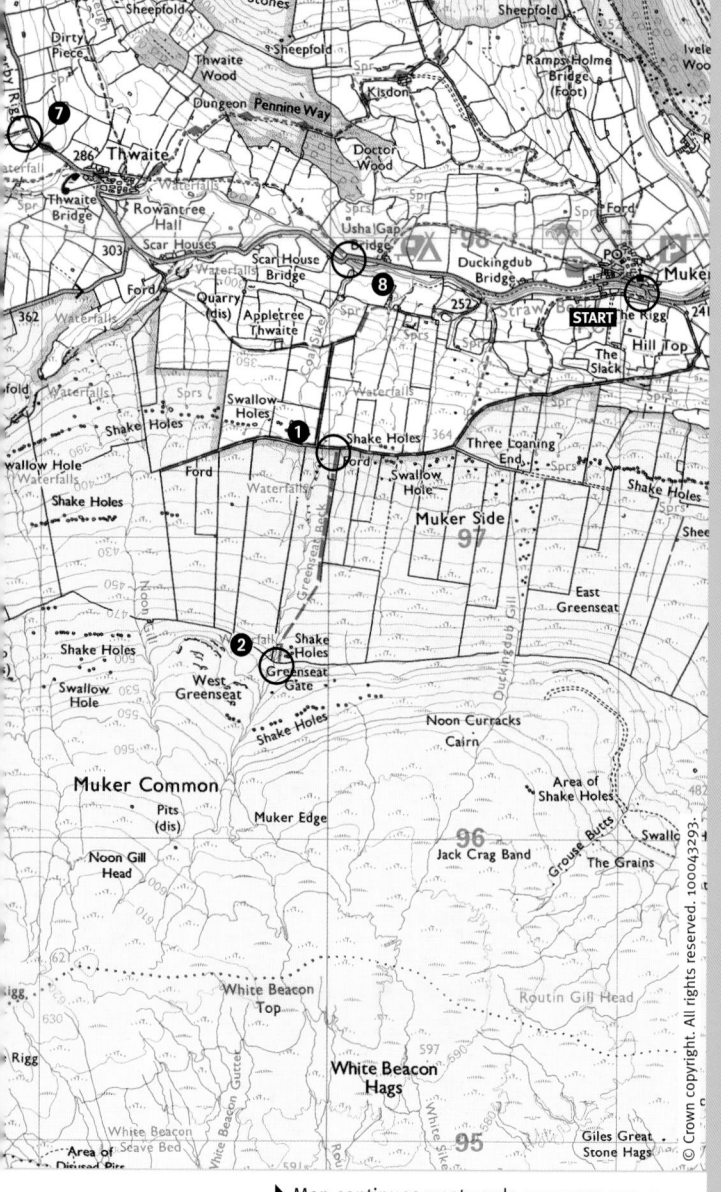

▶ Map continues westwards on pages 102–3

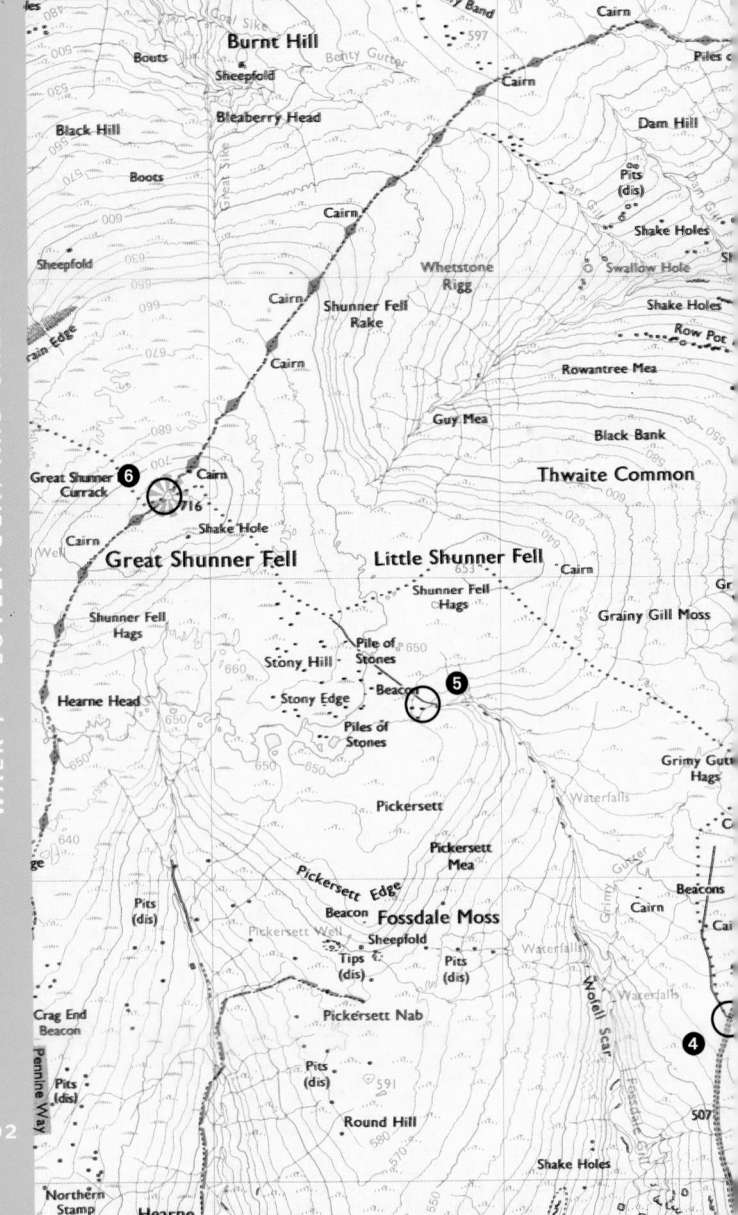

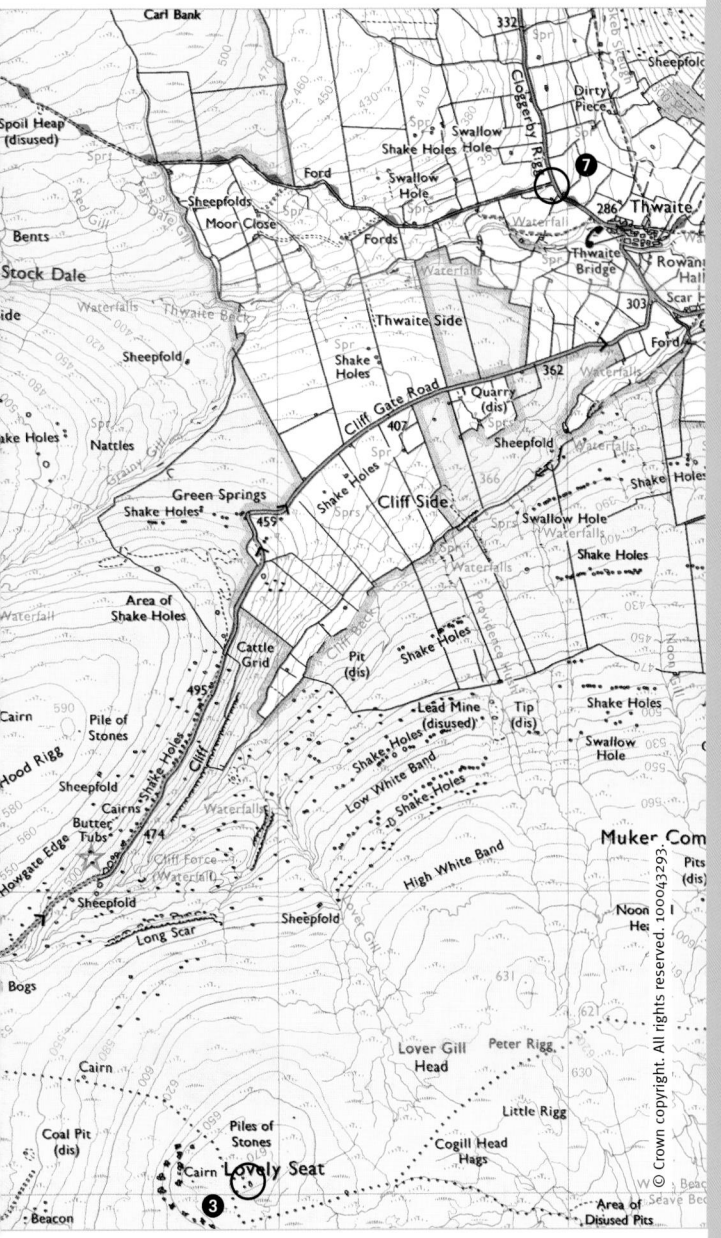

open moor, and continue up the left side of the gill, following a faint track.

■ The track to Greenseat Gate is a relic of the lead mining which used to take place on this part of the moor. You will be able to see an entrance to a level on the right of Greenseat Beck shortly after you arrive on the open moor.

▶ At the head of Greenseat Beck, cross the stream and head off across the open moor in a roughly south-west direction, aiming for the high ground. The bearing is about 240°. Once over the first hilltop (close to the point marked on the OS map as Peter Rigg), the summit of Lovely Seat should come into sight. Continue on the same bearing through the peaty groughs (natural ditches) at the head of Lover Gill.

■ Lover Gill has also seen lead mining, both in the eighteenth century and later in the nineteenth century. In his book *Swaledale, Its Mines and Smelt Mills*, Mike Gill

reports that 37 tons of lead ore were taken from Lover Gill between 1751 and 1755.

This area of moor has been 'gripped' – in other words, grips or channels have been cut to help drain the ground. Gripping has long been a feature of moorland management on grouse-shooting estates. In recent years, however, there has been some criticism from environmentalists of the effects of this technique. English Nature has pointed out that gripping reduces the number of blanket bogs, which provide important habitats in upland areas, and can also lead to a greater risk of flooding. In some moorland areas, grips have been deliberately blocked in order to restore bog habitats.

▶ After bashing through the tussocks, it's a relief to climb up the side of Lovely Seat and arrive at the summit ❸.

■ Lovely Seat is appropriately (if somewhat surprisingly) equipped with a stone seat

Buttertubs Pass from Kisdon Hill

where walkers can rest. This is one of those Dales summits where public access has only been legally possible since the introduction of access legislation in 2005.

Weather permitting, there are fine views south to all the Three Peaks: Penyghent is the most prominent landmark almost due south, while Ingleborough and Whernside are a little further to the west. Little Shunner Fell and (the next target for the walk) Great Shunner Fell are close at hand, over towards the north-west.

▶ From Lovely Seat, there is a momentary break from compass navigation to enjoy. Simply follow the fence line down the hillside to the cattle grid on the Hawes–Thwaite road ❹, at the Buttertubs Pass. The Buttertubs themselves, deep limestone potholes, are a little to the north of here.

From the road, the going becomes more challenging again. Indeed, the next section of moorland is perhaps the hardest

of the walk. The best route is to ignore the fences and to set a bearing initially of about 325°, as if heading for the summit of Little Shunner Fell. Keep the deep valley of Fossdale Gill below you, to your left. The ground climbs steadily, although Little Shunner Fell can be bypassed, leaving the actual summit slightly to the north. Aim for the main upper tributary into Fossdale Gill, which comes in from the north-west. At this point the bearing to follow changes to about 305°.

At the head of this upper gill, find the old stone wall that is shown on the OS map ❺. Here navigation becomes much more straightforward, even if the terrain is still rough. Follow the wall and (when it stops) the continuation fence. In due course, you will be brought straight to the summit of Great Shunner Fell ❻.

■ The OS has decided that the views from Great Shunner Fell are sufficiently impressive to be worthy of a symbol on its Explorer maps, and certainly on a good day this is a magnificent viewpoint. The view south, beyond Wensleydale to the Three Peaks, is now subtly different to the one enjoyed from Lovely Seat, while the high fells of the Howgills are close at hand to the south-west. Wainwright, however, had his eyes on a more distant horizon when he came this way: 'The real glory of the view is the western horizon, formed by a serrated range of peaks: the magic mountains of the Lake District, tremendously exciting even from afar,' he wrote.

The views northwards are also extensive, though the best views of Swaledale open up to the east during the long descent northwards off the summit of Great Shunner Fell. Birkdale Tarn, an artificial lake made from a smaller natural tarn to supply water

for the lead-mining industry, is a prominent landmark to the north.

▶ From Great Shunner Fell, the compass can be safely put away. The Pennine Way is paved almost all the way down the hillside to the main road near Thwaite ❼. Turn right when you meet the road.

Turn left in Thwaite and pick up the field footpath beside one of the last houses in the village. Continue straight ahead, while the Pennine Way turns left. This is a delightful path which runs through a set of meadows before rejoining the main valley road by Usha Gap Bridge ❽. Continue on the road for a few yards (metres), before turning left once more on to another footpath. After passing farm buildings, the path runs through further meadows and fields to emerge in Muker village.

Walking coast to coast

If walkers were to choose a footpath equivalent of, say, Hyde Park Corner or Spaghetti Junction, there would only be one real contender for where it would be. The footbridge over the Swale river at East Stonesdale near Keld doesn't seem like the centre of very much, but it is here that the two great English long-distance walking routes intersect. Here, for walkers, is the most important crossroads of them all.

The first to arrive was the Pennine Way, the pioneering route which took its inspiration from an idea first floated by journalist and outdoor-enthusiast Tom Stephenson in 1935, and which was finally officially opened in 1965. The stretch of the Pennine Way (Stephenson's 'long green trail') coming up from the south to the river crossing is one of the most beautiful on the whole route, skirting the side of Kisdon Hill high up above the Swale valley. To the north of the Swale footbridge, Pennine Way walkers have the satisfaction of knowing the welcoming bar at the Tan Hill Inn (see page 119) is little more than a hour away across the moors.

These days, however, more walkers arrive at East Stonesdale from a different direction, following the route of the Coast to Coast Walk from St Bees Head in Cumbria to Robin Hood's Bay in the North York Moors. The Coast to Coast Walk, now one of the most popular long-distance paths, is a fitting memorial to its creator, Alfred Wainwright.

Wainwright (the surname seems so much more appropriate to use than his first name) has a celebrated place in British outdoor life for the magnificent handbooks he produced about his beloved Lakeland fells. Originally from Blackburn, Wainwright moved north to Kendal in 1941 and began working for the local authority there. He became borough treasurer in 1948 and

This way to the sea

researched his seven Lakeland books in his spare time during the 1950s and early 1960s.

It was when he came to retire in 1967 that Wainwright had the opportunity of going a little further afield. He walked the whole of the Pennine Way, tackling it mainly through a series of day walks, and then began to have ideas of plotting his own route, somewhere else in the north. As he later explained, 'I wanted the starting point and finishing point to be exactly defined and not a source of doubt: the obvious choices were the high-tide levels of the two seas bordering the north of England.'

So Wainwright pulled out a ruler and map. The route, he said, almost chose itself: St Bees Head near Whitehaven, 'the most spectacular point on the western seaboard', to 'the quaint and attractive resort' of Robin Hood's Bay in the east. As Wainwright explained, 'the ruler passed through three national parks – the Lake District, the Yorkshire Dales and the North York Moors – and three quarters of the distance lay within the boundaries of these areas of outstanding beauty. And nowhere along this line was there an industrial blemish.'

But, as Wainwright admitted, the detail took rather longer to work out. He checked the full set of Ordnance Survey maps and came up with a route which, he claimed, made use of rights of way and open access land. And then he walked his new route and published a guidebook.

It was only when the Coast to Coast Walk had been given its first public airing in this way that Wainwright's choice of route began to get him into trouble. West of Kirkby Stephen, for example, he had taken the walk across the limestone pavement of Orton Scar and then down to Sunbiggin Tarn. 'I had no doubt that there was no right of way across the scar and that I had trespassed on private land, but relied on the general acceptance by northern landowners of open access over high uncultivated land . . . I was soon to be disillusioned.'

Wainwright's problem was that he was anticipating by more than thirty years the passing of the Countryside and Rights of Way Act 2000 and the introduction of rights which would give access to some of the open countryside which he wanted his readers to enjoy. Wainwright was familiar with the *de facto* access rights which had applied for generations over much of the Lakeland fells; unfortunately, however, the same approach did not apply in other parts of the north. A year or so after the guidebook to the Coast to Coast Walk first appeared, Wainwright received an admonishment from a local farmer who complained that walkers were entering his private land. A little later, things got even more problematic: the Country Landowners' Association added their voice to the protest, while the farmer fought back by grazing a bull on land crossed by Wainwright's route. Wainwright, who was not a man renowned for his tact or diplomacy, was forced to back down and redirect walkers off the fells on to nearby country roads. He did this, he said later, 'with many fervent damns and blasts'.

The Coast to Coast Walk is now an official national trail, and as a result a few other, relatively minor, changes to Wainwright's initial route have been put in place. In its broad design, however, the Coast to Coast Walk remains as Wainwright first designed it, a natural classic.

Incidentally, Wainwright was adamant that the correct way to do the walk was, as he did it, west to east. This way, he said, the prevailing winds would be behind walkers, not in their faces. But Wainwright had a further, rather more idiosyncratic, reason: walking from right to left on the map was abnormal, he argued. We write left to right, he pointed out. We should follow the Coast to Coast Walk left to right as well.

WALK 8

ROGAN'S SEAT

DIFFICULTY 👟 👟 👟 👟

DISTANCE 8½ miles (13.7 km)

KELD — PENNINE WAY — EAST GILL — ROGAN'S SEAT — SWINNER GILL — CRACKPOT HALL — KELD

MAP OS Explorer OL30, Yorkshire Dales (Northern and Central) or Harveys Dales North

STARTING POINT Keld (GR 893012)

PUBLIC TRANSPORT Buses run Monday–Saturday from Reeth and Richmond, and on Tuesdays from Hawes. Services from Darlington/Hawes on summer Sundays/Bank Holidays and from Leeds/Wakefield on some summer Sundays/Bank Holidays go as far as Thwaite, 2 miles (3 km) away. (Check for winter services.)

PARKING Car park in Keld

Tracks and footpaths for most of the way, but with about 1½ miles (2.5 km) of walking on open ground, where navigation is necessary.

■ Keld, like other villages in Swaledale, was a centre not only of lead mining but also of hand knitting. Knitting was enormously important in the northern Yorkshire Dales for over three centuries, not as a hobby but as a key additional source of money for the inhabitants. Knitting was undertaken by men just as much as by women, and children too would be expected to learn to knit very early so that they could contribute their share of income to the household.

Despite the skill involved, knitting was extremely poorly paid – perhaps a few pence for a pair of hand-knitted stockings. To make any profit at all, the Dales knitters would frequently work all day and miners sometimes knitted on their way to and from the lead mines. They also worked exceptionally fast. The standard technique was to keep the right-hand needle in a wooden sheath which was tucked into a belt worn around the waist. This meant that only the minimum of needle movement was required. 'Keep short needles,' children were told, when learning their craft. Dales knitters developed a regular swaying motion, moving their arms rhythmically up and down as stitches were knitted. The needles themselves were made of wire and were curved.

The hand-knitting industry began to go into decline during the second half of the nineteenth century, unfortunately just at the time when lead mining was also suffering economically. The story of the Dales knitters has been recorded in Marie Hartley and Joan Ingilby's classic account, *The Old Hand-Knitters of the Dales*, first published in 1951. Their conclusion is that 'the former importance of hand-knitting as a branch of the textile industry to the economic survival of people with few resources living in the high lands of the Yorkshire Dales cannot be overemphasised'.

They also recount the tale of the Independent minister of Keld, Edward Stillman, who set off in 1820 to walk to London to collect money to rebuild his chapel. As he walked the roads, he did what almost everyone in his village would have done – he knitted.

▶ From Keld walk down to East Stonesdale bridge (see page 108). Beyond, turn left following the waymarks of the Pennine Way past East Stonesdale Farm. Continue climbing, passing the small settlement of West Stonesdale away to the left and Frith Lodge to the right.

At the second old barn you pass ❶, leave the Pennine Way to follow the moorside wall uphill. Keep to the left-hand side of Mould Gill, making for the high ground of Tarn Rigg.

■ The upper pastures and moorland adjacent to the Pennine Way are home each spring to numerous pairs of lapwings, who breed in pasture and wet grassland. Lapwings are widely known as peewits, in reference to the bird's display call. In the Yorkshire Dales, however, lapwings traditionally bear another, slightly different name – the tewit.

▶ As the ground levels out, the water of little Frith Tarn will come into sight. Pass to the north of the tarn, in order to find the place where you can easily cross over a moorland fence. The valley of East Gill will open up below,

▶ page 118

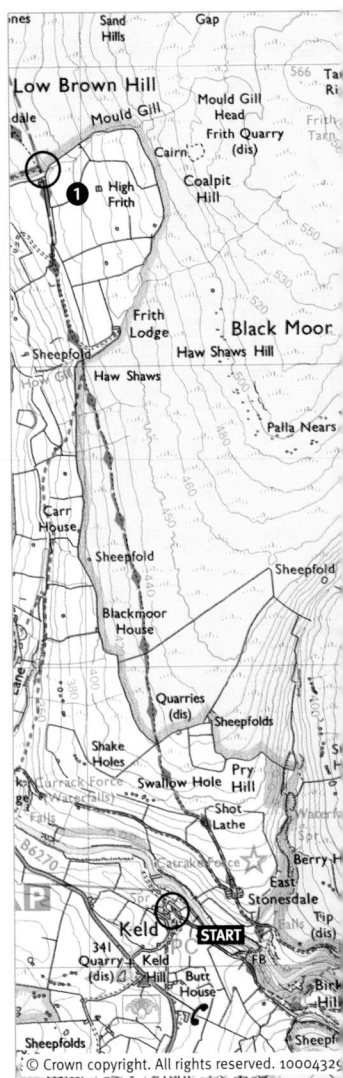

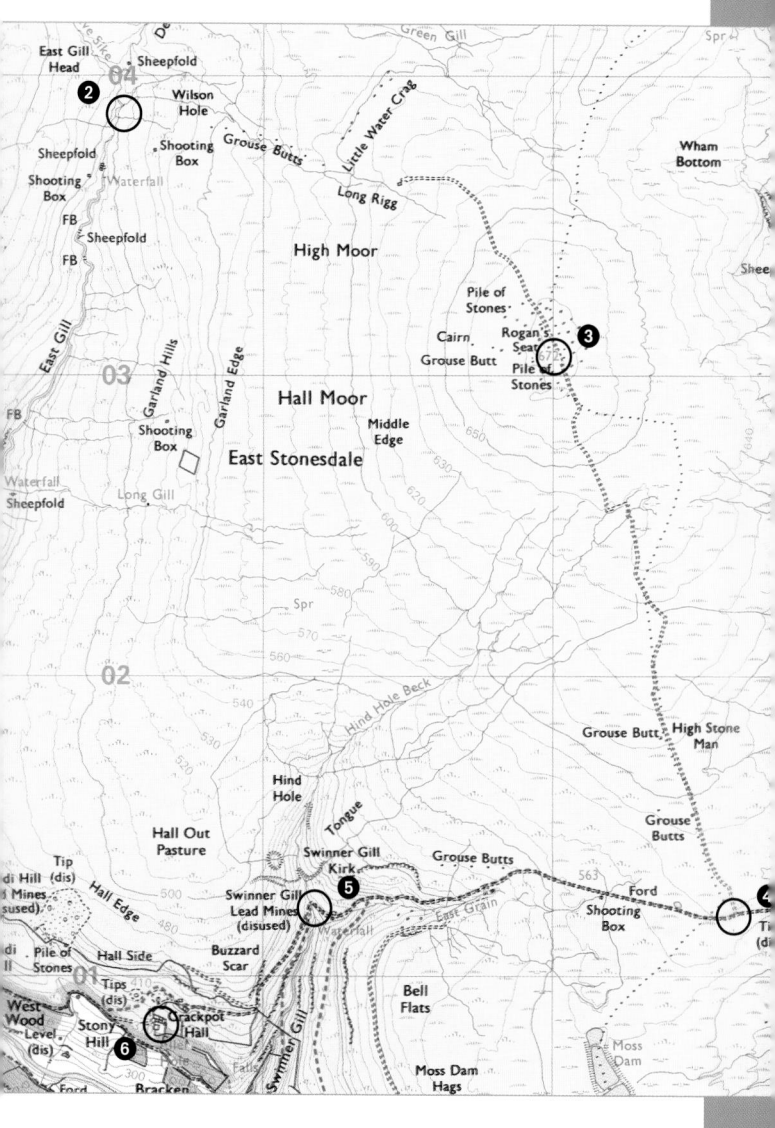

View of Swaledale from Crackpot Hall

with the high ground of Water Crag (to the left) and Rogan's Seat (right) beyond. Head down to the valley at the point where several streams converge, and cross the infant river ❷.

From here, find a path up the side of the first valley coming in from the east, keeping the valley to your right. If in doubt as to which clough to select, look out for the prominent rock which conveniently is to be found at the bottom.

Halfway up the valley, there is a line of grouse butts and a path between them that makes walking easier. Continue up this path. At the top, the path becomes a grassy track and finally a surfaced shooting track. Take the track up to Rogan's Seat ❸.

■ Rogan's Seat is a plateau, without an obvious summit. Although slightly higher than neighbouring Water Crag, it is the latter which has been given the trig point (visible over to the north-east).

It has to be admitted that not everyone is particularly impressed by what they find when they reach Rogan's Seat:

the 'most boring 2000ft hill in England', according to one author. But if the summit itself is unspectacular, there are fine views to enjoy on the gentle descent southwards on the shooting track. Great Shunner Fell and Lovely Seat (Walk 7) lie across the Swale valley, while between them, further away, is the top of Great Knoutberry. Even further away, towards the south, it may be possible to spot Great Whernside.

▶ The shooting track offers a pleasant and easy walk off Rogan's Seat across the grouse moorland of Gunnerside Moor. After well over 1 mile (approaching 2 km), the track meets up with the track from Swinner Gill to Gunnerside. Turn right here ❹.

From this point, it is an easy descent into Swinner Gill (see page 94), taking the route followed by Walk 6 in reverse. Leave the shooting track to take the well-walked footpath down East Grain gill to the ruins of the smelt mill and dressing floor ❺.

Continue past Crackpot Hall ❻, and return to Keld over the bridge at East Stonesdale.

The pub on the hill

It is the sheer improbability of it all that gives the Tan Hill Inn its reputation. This is a pub which is miles from anywhere, on the top of a windswept hill, with only sheep (who are not renowned for buying many rounds of drinks) for neighbours. It's not even as though Tan Hill itself is – let's be blunt – a particularly attractive hilltop.

In business terms, therefore, Tan Hill would seem to be easy to write off, an obvious no-hoper. And this, perversely, is perhaps the secret of its success. One reason why the pub attracts such feelings of warmth is that it has managed to keep its front door open for visitors, day after day, despite being assaulted on two fronts: by the harsh winds of the Pennines and by the cold logic of economics.

Most people who find their way to Tan Hill drive to it, either up the empty road from Keld, or up the empty road from Brough or up the equally empty Arkengarthdale road. But for walkers, the classic approach to the pub is from the south by means of the Pennine Way (the route recommended for Walk 9 in this book). In good weather, the path offers the opportunity to appreciate just how wide and lonely are the expanses of Stonesdale Moor, before the hill brow is reached and the pub abruptly appears, all by itself, in the middle distance ahead. But when the cloud is down (and it comes down frequently here), the first glimpse of Tan Hill as the building looms up out of the whiteness can seem nothing short of miraculous.

For more than twenty years from the mid-1980s, Tan Hill was home to a redoubtable couple, Alec (or, to be more correct, Alex) and Margaret Baines. The story of how they became the owners was retold by them many times, to everyone from casual visitors to foreign television crews: how they were living in a cottage in Gargrave near Settle and doing a little farming near Malham, how they first heard about the sale of Tan Hill on the news, how they joked about putting in an offer, how they found themselves at the auction and how the auctioneer began proceedings with the words, 'I'm looking for eccentrics'. Their bid of £82,500 won the day. Locals initially thought they'd be out after a year.

Tan Hill was at a very low ebb at this time. The pub was, for a time, getting through new landlords at the rate of one a year and the auction of England's highest pub was in danger of becoming a regular on journalists' calendars, a standard feature of the summer silly season. When the Baines took possession of their new purchase, its electricity was supplied by a generator which was prone to breaking down and the only water came from a nearby spring. The water supply sometimes only produced a pint of water an hour, hardly enough for a functioning pub or indeed for a family of five – and the Baines moved in with their three daughters, at that time aged eleven, seven and two. They washed once a week, all in the same water.

Or at least that's how Margaret has told the story. There is a problem when writing about Tan Hill that hard facts can sometimes be elusive, liable to be blown away as soon as the front door is opened and the bar left behind. According to Tan Hill's own official website, the Baines bought the pub in 1986. David Gerrard's affectionate portrait of the pub, *In the Winds of Heaven*, published in 1991, also states firmly that the auction took place in August 1986. This seems pretty conclusive. But ask Margaret Baines now about that auction date and a lengthy discussion with her youngest daughter Kim (now in her early twenties) is the outcome. Doubts begin to emerge – was the auction 1986? Perhaps it was actually 1985? Yes, surely it must have been September 1985?

What's not in doubt is what happened to the family during their first winter. They were snow-bound for six weeks. The beer froze in the pipes. Drinking water came from melted snow ('it's surprising how much snow you have to melt for very little water'). And, of course, there was hardly much passing trade to help the Baines build up their new business.

Despite the early set-backs, the Baines' formula for Tan Hill seemed to work. The bar was, effectively, their living room. They opened the front door when they got up and kept the bar open until it was time to go to bed again. In between, anyone who found themselves at the door was welcome inside.

And, increasingly, more and more people did appear at the door. It helped when, in 1990, a new side wing with seven en-suite bedrooms was added. Tan Hill became an obvious destination for coach parties and for such events as motor rallies and biker gatherings. The pub was also pressed into use as a location for films (Kevin Costner was here once, all dressed up, for *Robin Hood: Prince of Thieves*) and for television commercials (the famous double-glazing advert with Ted Moult back in the 1980s was the first of several). There were days when Margaret Baines found she was supplying 150 meals from the kitchen. Fortunately, Tan Hill's kitchen is equipped with five large freezers, just in case the snows come back unexpectedly.

So all in all Alec and Margaret Baines had reason to be proud of what they had achieved in their pub high up on the Pennine hills when they finally decided, in the summer of 2005, that it was time for retirement. The Tan Hill, of course, remains open under new landlords, ready to welcome the new generation of Pennine Wayfarers who come staggering up the hill from Keld. Margaret Baines, however, has already started to plan a new project: a book of memoirs commemorating her twenty-odd years at the pub. The working title? – 'You get less time for murder.'

WALK 9

TAN HILL AND RAVENSEAT

DIFFICULTY 👢 👢 👢 **DISTANCE** 10½ miles (17 km)

KELD   PENNINE WAY   TAN HILL   RAVENSEAT   KELD

MAP OS Explorer OL30, Yorkshire Dales (Northern and Central) or OS Explorer OL19, Howgill Fells and Upper Eden Valley. Alternatively, Harveys Dales North.

STARTING POINT Keld (GR 893012)

PUBLIC TRANSPORT Buses run Monday–Saturday from Reeth and Richmond, and on Tuesdays from Hawes. Services from Darlington/Hawes on summer Sundays/Bank Holidays and from Leeds/Wakefield on some summer Sundays/Bank Holidays go as far as Thwaite, 2 miles (3 km) away. (Check for winter services.)

PARKING In the car park in Keld

A route which, although it makes use throughout of footpaths and tracks, offers the experience of walking wild and empty moors and as such surely merits inclusion in a 'freedom to roam' guide.

▶ From Keld walk down to East Stonesdale bridge and pick up the Pennine Way running north, taking the route also initially followed by Walk 8.

The Pennine Way crosses Lad Gill stream on a modern bridge ❶ and then climbs some more, towards Lad Gill Hill. The path can be, in Wainwright's words, 'juicy' underfoot.

■ Visibility permitting, the very distinctive cairns on Nine Standards Rigg (Walk 10) will come into sight 1 mile (1.6 km) or so before you reach Tan Hill. Nine Standards Rigg is at this point almost directly due west.

Ahead are the hills of the north Pennines, including Mickle Fell to the north-west. Mickle Fell was, at 2591 ft (788 m), Yorkshire's highest peak until local government reorganization in 1974 took it away from Yorkshire and gave it to County Durham. Some Yorkshire folk still like to claim the peak as rightfully theirs.

▶ Continue on the Pennine Way towards the Tan Hill Inn ❷.

■ Although the Tan Hill Inn (see page 119) today stands alone on the moors, it is not here by accident. Tan Hill was important in times past as a centre for drovers

bringing cattle south from Scotland. A number of old droving routes spread out from the inn.

An even more significant influence on Tan Hill's history was coal, which for centuries was taken from the moorland here. The first record of coal mining at Tan Hill dates back to 1296, but the industry may be even older than this.

Richmond Castle received coal dug from Tan Hill in the fourteenth century, and three hundred years later Lady Anne Clifford (see page 156) also took Tan Hill coal to warm herself in Pendragon Castle. Over the years coal from Tan Hill has helped keep houses warm in Appleby, Penrith, Kirkby Stephen and much of Swaledale and Wensleydale. It has also helped fire the lead-smelting mills in the area.

The Tan Hill coal seam varies in thickness, reaching a maximum of approximately $3\frac{1}{2}$ ft (about 1 m) in the Kings Pit area to the east. But the land on either side of the

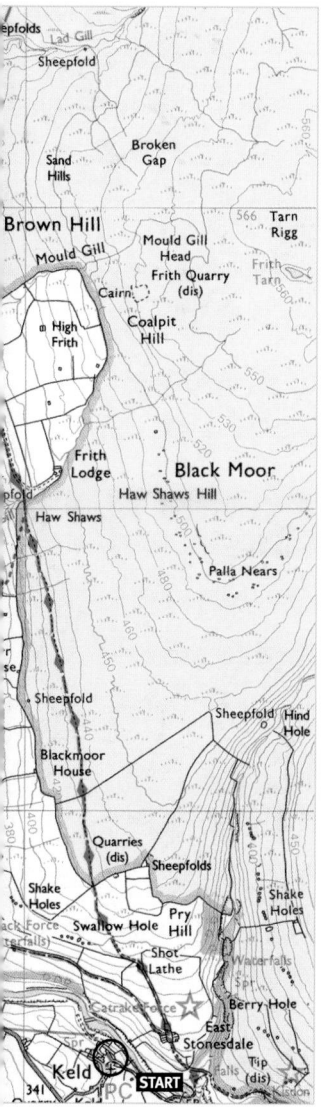

Pennine Way was also an important mining area where a number of deep shafts were sunk. Coal was extracted, too, via a level which was driven through the hillside from Mould Gill, 1 mile (1.6 km) or so south of Tan Hill. The site of the level is just off the Pennine Way and marked on OS maps.

Although known as Tan Hill colliery, this wasn't a colliery of the type which became familiar in the twentieth century. Coal was taken at Tan Hill primarily by means of shafts sunk in the moor, which in many cases eventually came to be interconnected. The shafts today pose a real hazard, since many are not capped. Margaret Baines formerly of the Tan Hill Inn tells the recent tale of a sheepdog which fell to its death down an old shaft that had become hidden by vegetation. Despite the fact that this area has now been declared access land, it is not a good idea to start wandering off the established paths hereabouts.

▶ Map continues northwards on page 126

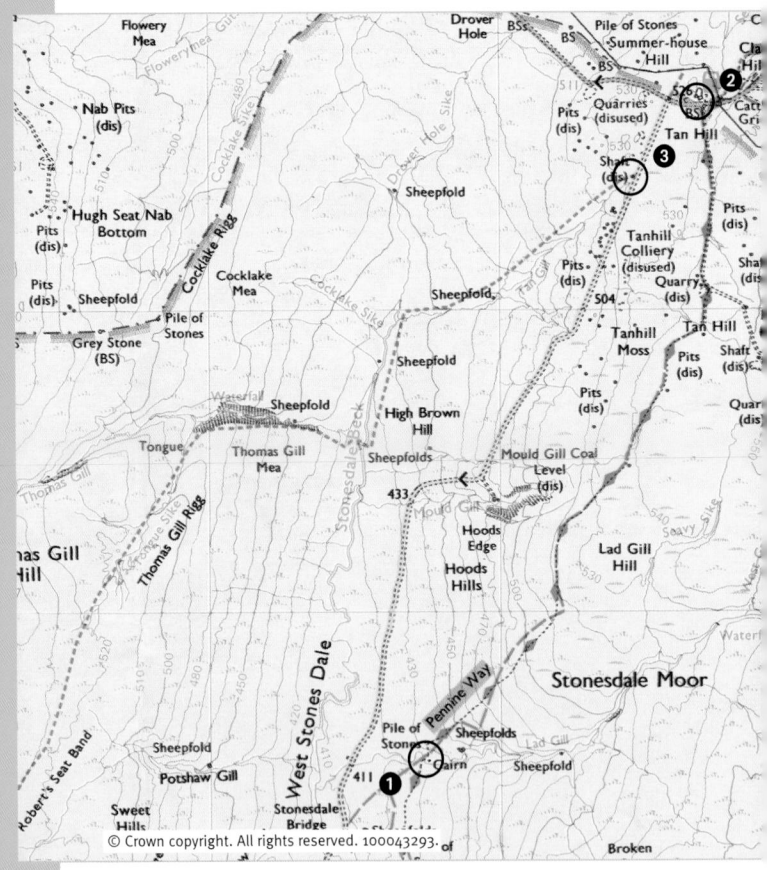

After centuries of mining, the tradition petered out following the First World War and the last Tan Hill coal was removed in 1938. The same coal seam (which carries the generic name of 'Tan Hill' coal) was also mined elsewhere in the Dales, including at Blakethwaite in Gunnerside Gill (Walk 6) and on the flanks of Great Shunner Fell (Walk 7).

Coal mining ceased at Tan Hill just as an era of a different kind was ending at the inn. During much of the early decades of the twentieth century, the landlady was the formidable Susan Peacock, a no-nonsense Yorkshirewoman who, it is said, kept a gun at hand just in case it was needed. Tan Hill was her home for over thirty years. Shortly before her death in 1937, she was 'discovered' by the BBC and made a number of radio broadcasts.

▶ From Tan Hill Inn walk back down the Keld road for a short way, taking the footpath off to the right which heads down to Stonesdale Beck ❸.

Follow the path as it climbs up the side of deeply cut Thomas Gill and then runs along a pleasant plateau ridge close to Robert's Seat. Eventually the footpath drops down to the small farming settlement of Ravenseat.

■ Isolated Ravenseat was described as a village in the eighteenth century, when a small community lived here. The stone bridge recalls the former packhorse route which ran between here and the town of Kirkby Stephen.

▶ As you approach Ravenseat, turn left just before the path fords the Whitsundale Beck, entering a field. Pass close to farm buildings ❹, then pick up the field footpath which runs along the east side of the river valley. The path offers a fine view down to the deep gorge cut by the river near Oven Mouth.

Leave the moor to pass close to the ruins of Smithy Holme ❺ and find the lower footpath which runs along on a pleasant terrace above the Swale. Return to Keld from Park Bridge by the road.

The Kaber Rigg uprising

If you were launching an uprising to overthrow the Crown, you might ideally choose a better place to assemble your forces than the lonely windswept moor of Kaber Rigg, north of the Nine Standards (Walk 10) and east of Kirkby Stephen. You might also, let's be honest, want more than twenty or so horsemen and a handful of foot soldiers.

Captain Robert Atkinson and the small group of co-conspirators who joined him on Kaber Rigg on the night of Monday 12 October 1663 did not, however, initially feel too isolated. Many others, they knew, shared their loathing of the political settlement in London, which in 1660 had brought Charles II back to the throne that his father had lost so dramatically eleven years earlier. Many others, like them, were determined to bring back the days of the English Commonwealth. Indeed, 12 October 1663 was the day which had been chosen for these groups to rise up together and start to fight back. This was the day fixed for what historians now describe (albeit usually only briefly or in footnotes) as the Northern Risings.

It is hardly surprising that the restoration of the monarchy wasn't welcomed by everyone. England had just passed through a period of both civil war and revolution, a time of extraordinary change when both spiritual and temporal authority was challenged. The established church with all its wealth and power found itself competing with new democratic forms of Christianity, promoted by itinerant lay preachers in sects such as the Baptists, Anabaptists and Quakers. They had read the Bible for themselves and used it to call for social upheaval. God, they said, was no longer to be reached only through the mediation of priests, and they even suggested that human society could be reshaped in God's image, to be for the benefit of all, not just the rich.

This was heady stuff and it frightened many middle-of-the-road Parliamentarians as much as it did those who had backed the Royalist cause. By 1660, Parliament had come to the conclusion that the restoration of the monarchy (this time, though, at Parliament's behest rather than by divine right) offered the best chance of re-imposing order.

As after any revolutionary period, authority was re-established harshly. Most of the army was disbanded, leaving carefully selected and purged regiments in place as garrisons in key cities. Under the Corporation Act of 1661 dissenters were removed from positions of responsibility in civic life, and power was increasingly placed in the hands of local JPs, inevitably men of property. The Act of Settlement of 1662 put restrictions on travel by ordinary people, something which had been a feature of the liberty of the revolutionary years. Meanwhile, the Church of England was also purged of its radical elements. The bishops were given back their lands, powers and seats in the House of Lords, while dissenting ministers were expelled from their posts. In Yorkshire, over fifty ministers were removed as dissenters.

It seems that the plot which produced the October 1663 rising was led by a group of dissenting ministers and former officers in Parliament's army. Robert Atkinson, who led the Kaber Rigg group, was a yeoman from Mallerstang who had risen through the army ranks, first as a trooper, then as a quartermaster and a lieutenant, until he became commander of the troops of Westmorland county. For a time during the Commonwealth period he was Governor of Appleby. Another conspirator, Robert's namesake John Atkinson, came from Askrigg in Wensleydale. John Atkinson was a stockinger by trade (a merchant trading in the knitted goods produced in the Dales) and an Anabaptist in his beliefs.

Captain Robert Atkinson had been present at meetings held in Harrogate during the early part of 1663, when the plot for the uprising was developed. The host for these meetings was an Independent minister called Edward Richardson, who had held the post of Dean of Ripon before being ejected three years earlier. The conspirators came from across the Yorkshire area and the north, and were in touch with like-minded rebels in Scotland and the south. One of their leaders travelled down to London in order to synchronize their efforts on the chosen date of 12 October. In the event, however, the London group tried to postpone the rising, leaving the north to go it alone.

Robert Atkinson roped in his brother-in-law, Robert Waller, to assist him at the Westmorland end. Their plan appears to have been to rendezvous in Kirkby Stephen and then to move on to Appleby, to free prisoners and to seize the town's excise. Atkinson had promised that Thomas Fairfax, the old Civil War general, would be there to lead the rebels, but the promise was rooted more in wishful thinking than in reality: Fairfax had far more political nous than to support the uprising. The reinforcements Atkinson had expected would join his team from Kendal and Scotland also failed to materialize. Eventually, after waiting until shortly after midnight on Kaber Rigg, Atkinson told his men to disperse. The weather that day was reportedly poor, with heavy rain, and it must have been a long, cold evening on the moor.

Atkinson's fellow conspirators had not fared much better elsewhere. The plans for risings in Durham and Northallerton were aborted and the biggest gathering of rebels, which took place at Farnley Wood, failed in its intention of capturing nearby Leeds. As at Kaber Rigg the men eventually dispersed, believing that their actions had escaped the attention of the authorities.

Unfortunately, however, Yorkshire's High Sheriff Sir Thomas Gower knew all about their plans. One of the ringleaders had turned informer, and Gower (who also had his own network of spies and informers) had been aware for many weeks that 12 October was the date selected for the uprising. In the aftermath many of the participants were brought to trial, and twenty-four were executed. Robert Atkinson's brother-in-law, Robert Waller, was executed along with two associates in Appleby in March 1664, while Robert Atkinson himself met the same fate the following September. Atkinson remained defiant to the end.

If Kaber Rigg and the other uprisings appear in retrospect doomed, they nevertheless reflected the strong anti-Restoration feeling which existed in many parts of the north of England at the time. But the question remained as to whether the participants had unwittingly allowed themselves to be used as stooges by the government, which was then able to use the failure of the rising to strengthen its control. Some of Gower's spies, it seems, may have taken on the role of *agent provocateur*. The real plot, some later argued, was not the one drawn up by Robert Atkinson and his associates – it was a government plot.

WALK 10

NINE STANDARDS

DIFFICULTY 👟 👟 👟   **DISTANCE** 9½ miles (15 km)

| KIRKBY STEPHEN | LADTHWAITE | HARTLEY FELL | NINE STANDARDS RIGG | HARTLEY FELL | HARTLEY | KIRKBY STEPHEN |

MAP OS Explorer OL19, Howgill Fells and Upper Eden Valley, or Harveys Dales North

STARTING POINT Kirkby Stephen town centre (GR 775085)

PUBLIC TRANSPORT Buses serve Kirkby Stephen (Monday–Saturday) from Kendal and Sedbergh (route 564) and Penrith and Appleby (route 563). There is also a local community bus service, Plusbus. Kirkby Stephen station (Settle–Carlisle line) is about 1⅓ mile (2 km) from the town centre; the station is served by buses on route 564 and the Plusbus.

PARKING In Kirkby Stephen

The Nine Standards cairns high on the hilltop above Kirkby Stephen are one of the most impressive landmarks in this part of the north of England. This walk primarily follows the well-trodden route of the Coast to Coast Walk, with the option of some rougher walking in open country. Nine Standards Rigg is exposed in poor weather.

▶ Leave Kirkby Stephen town centre by the road to Hawes.

(The road junction here is unusual in offering a signpost which gives distances in both miles and furlongs. For those who need reminding, there are eight furlongs to the mile.)

After the road junction, continue along the Hawes road for a couple of furlongs (a few hundred yards or metres, if you insist). As the road narrows, turn diagonally left down a well-signed bridleway. This sunken lane quickly emerges beside the edge of the River Eden at a little wooden footbridge, known locally as Swingy Bridge ❶.

■ Just before the bridge is a carved stone with a short poem by Meg Peacocke. The stone marks the start of Kirkby Stephen's Poetry Path, which has unexpectedly become one of the town's popular visitor attractions.

It was in the difficult time in the aftermath of the 2001 foot and mouth outbreak that the East Cumbria Countryside Project commissioned Meg Peacocke to write a set of twelve short poems, each representing a month in the life of a hill farmer. The idea was to commemorate and celebrate the role which farmers play in this part of Cumbria as custodians of the landscape. Meg Peacocke was an inspired choice for the venture: she is an established poet and poetry tutor who has published a number of collections of her work, she lives in Mallerstang just to the south of Kirkby Stephen and she also keeps a smallholding.

The poem that you will find beside the Swingy Bridge represents the month of January. February's poem is situated a little way beyond the bridge, next to a stone barn. It reads:

Snowlight peers at the
  byre door.
Neither day nor night.
Four months ago we
  fetched the cattle in,
safe from reiving wind
  and rain,
months of standing and
  shifting, burdened
with patience. When will
  winter end?

▶ page 138

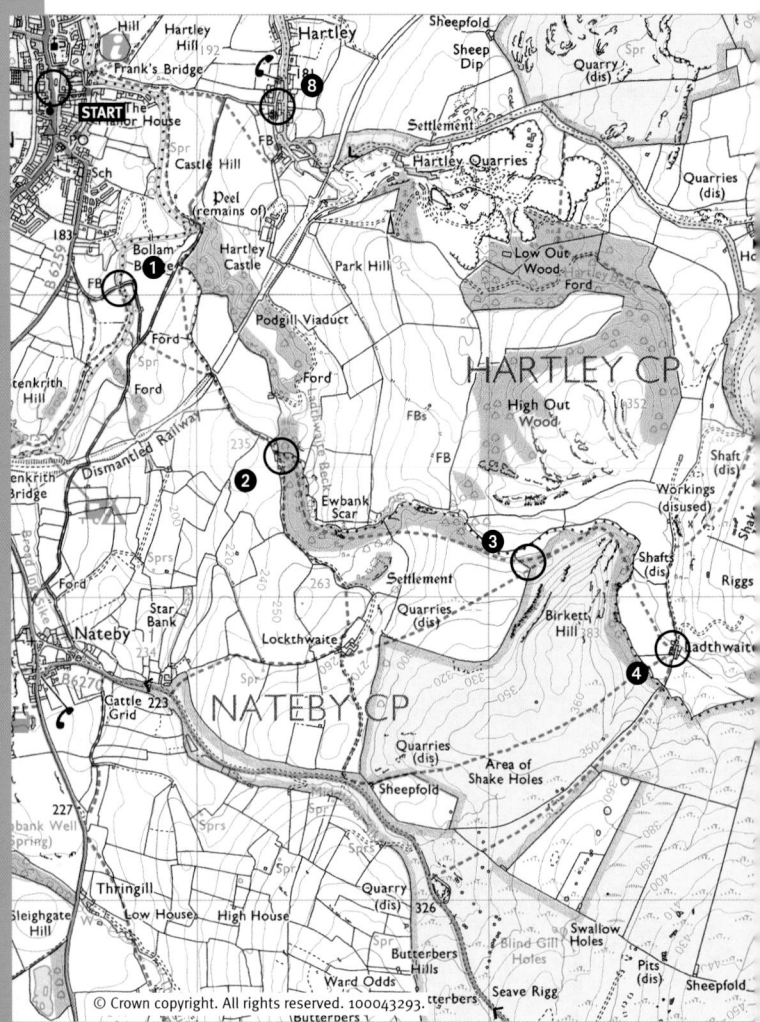

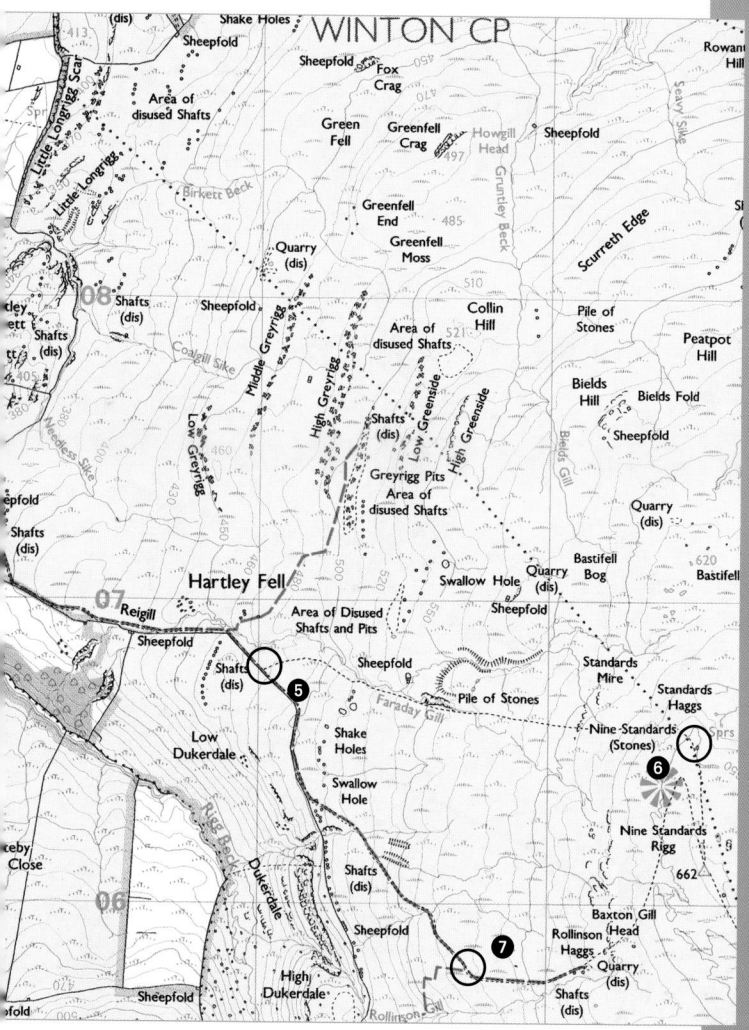

*Thin strokes of sun on the
    byre floor.
Fork a load of silage out,
    straighten your back to
    watch them shove
their muzzles in, and
    wonder if they crave
the hazy nights when they
    can roam
among tall summer
    grasses, sleek and sound
    and warm.*

Pip Hall, a lettering artist
now living in Dentdale, had
the skilled job of carving the
poems on to blocks of stone
selected from a local quarry.
The Poetry Path opened in
the summer of 2004.

The poems for March to
December lie off this route,
but there is an illustrated
booklet available from Kirkby
Stephen's tourist information
centre for those interested
in completing the full
Poetry Path.

▶ Continue a short distance
along the bridleway from Swingy
Bridge. When the path meets
another bridleway continue
straight ahead, over a stile, to

follow a faint footpath up the
hill. At the top there is a bridge
over the dismantled Stainmore
branch railway.

■ Kirkby Stephen was once
served by two railway lines
and two stations. In 1861,
a generation before the
Settle–Carlisle line was
pushed through the hills
to Kirkby Stephen by the
Midland Railway, the South
Durham and Lancashire Union
Railway reached the town.

This first line provided
a trans-Pennine route over
Stainmore summit from
County Durham, via Barnard
Castle and Bowes, to the
north-west main line at Tebay.
The line was built primarily
for freight traffic, as a way
of taking coal from Teeside to
the north-west and iron ore
back from the north-west to
Teeside. However, passengers
also used the line and there
were popular summer specials
including through Newcastle–
Blackpool expresses.

The railway closed in 1962.
The 1 mile (1.6 km) or so of
trackbed south-east of Kirkby

Stephen has now been acquired by the Northern Viaduct Trust, a charity which restores and maintains important disued railway viaducts. One of these is Podgill viaduct, a very short distance to the north along the trackbed, which has been given Grade II listed status.

▶ Follow the footpath beyond the railway. When the path turns left, turn left again over a stile ❷ to find the attractive footpath which wanders through the woods beside Ladthwaite Beck. The waterfall below Ewbank Scar is a particular delight.

Eventually the path emerges from the woods below Birkett Hill ❸. Turn left immediately, into a neighbouring field. At this point, open access country begins.

From here, one route is to scramble up to the top of Birkett Hill (aim initially a little south of the hill, to find the rusty metal gate which will give access through the fence). Continue south-eastwards beyond the hill until you meet a fell wall. Follow this to the north, to find the footpath to Ladthwaite.

Alternatively, those who prefer to save their energy for later can simply follow the footpath around the bottom of Birkett Hill, to arrive at Ladthwaite ❹.

■ Ladthwaite is an attractive farmhouse bearing the familiar -thwaite suffix, which comes from the Norse for a clearing. Red squirrels live in the woods near by.

▶ From Ladthwaite, follow the right of way northwards, along the farm lane. Turn right, to pick up the long-distance Coast to Coast Walk coming up from Kirkby Stephen and Hartley. Follow the track up across Hartley Fell to the footpath sign ❺ which points the concessionary path to Nine Standards. Take this (slightly boggy) path up to the hill brow ❻.

■ After a number of false summits and modern outlying cairns, the Nine Standards finally appear. These cairns, a much-loved landmark locally, have stood high on the hillside for many years. Exactly how many years, however, is a matter of some dispute.

In *A Coast to Coast Walk*, Wainwright makes do with the suitably vague 'They are certainly old', before retelling the romantic tale that the cairns were built to give Scottish marauders venturing into the upper Eden valley the false idea that an army of English were encamped on the hilltop.

In fact, a recent study suggests that the cairns that we see today may be relatively modern, perhaps no more than two hundred years old – though, if this is the case, the cairns probably replaced earlier landmarks on the hilltop. The name Nine Standards appeared on eighteenth-century maps.

Over the years, the cairns have needed regular attention to prevent them collapsing. However, the plans made in 2005 by the East Cumbria Countryside Project for some serious restoration work to ensure the long-term survival of the Standards ran into

difficulties when legal approval was withheld. The cairns are listed monuments and while repair work is permitted, more substantial rebuilding is, it seems, a different matter.

▶ Continue along the brow of the hill from the Nine Standards to the viewing stone (the correct term is 'toposcope').

■ This toposcope was erected to commemorate the marriage between Prince Charles and Lady Diana. On a clear day, the views westwards to the Lakes are magnificent, from Blencathra in the north to the Conistone Old Man further south. Scafell Pike, England's highest peak, is also visible in the middle distance. It is said that on an exceptionally clear day you can see from here right across northern England, from the Irish Sea to the North Sea.

▶ Most people will want to continue beyond the toposcope to visit the Nine Standards Rigg trig point.

The well-walked path which disappears down the hillside before you reach the trig point offers the route back. (In very poor visibility, it may be difficult to find this path; in this situation, it may be preferable to return via the path used to reach the Nine Standards.)

The path drops quickly. At a footpath sign ❼, take the right-hand choice (signed Coast to Coast Walk) and follow this diagonally down the hillside, to meet up eventually with the fell wall. Rejoin the track taken on the outward journey, and continue as the track becomes a tarmacked road.

Keep to the road past Hartley quarry (the quarrying activity effectively means that it is not possible to use the footpath shown on the map through Low Out Wood).

■ The massive limestone quarry at Hartley is now operated by the company Cemex. Limestone quarried in the northern Pennines is mostly crushed for use as aggregate and roadstone.

▶ Find the footpath from pretty Hartley village ❽ back to Kirkby Stephen, crossing the River Eden by Frank's Bridge.

Blackcocks and greyhens

Walkers on the heather moors above Wensleydale and Swaledale are not likely to be short of the company of red grouse. It's because of the desire to increase the numbers of these birds, or more accurately to increase the shooting of these birds, that the northern heather moorlands are carefully managed by keepers from the large landowning estates.

The sighting of a black grouse is something much more unusual and much more special. Particularly exciting is the ceremony known as the lek, when the male birds show off and strut their stuff to impress the female birds. Watching a lek is an unforgettable experience, one of the greatest wildlife wonders which Britain has to offer.

There was a time when you could find black grouse all over Britain; at one stage they even bred in parts of Surrey. They hung on in the lowland heaths of Dorset and Hampshire until the 1930s and could still be found in Dartmoor and Exmoor until the late 1960s. But not now. The number of black grouse dropped rapidly during the second half of the last century and the bird became listed as an endangered species.

In 1995 a major national survey took place to locate the remaining black grouse. A very small breeding population was discovered in north and central Wales, together with a much larger population, several thousand strong, in Scotland. The survey also found a significant concentration of black grouse in the north Pennines area, where it has been estimated that perhaps 800–1700 'lekking' males are present. The southern edge of this territory includes the northern areas of the Yorkshire Dales.

The male black grouse, in particular, is an impressive creature, measuring about 21 inches (55 cm) from tip of bill to end of tail. Its plumage is primarily glossy black or blue-black, which gives the bird its folk name of 'blackcock', although it also has white bands on the wings which can be seen when it flies. Its most distinctive features, however, are the bright red patches above its eyes, which are known as wattles. During the lek, the birds have the ability to inflate these wattles so that they become even more distinctive.

The female or 'greyhen', by contrast, is more constrained in its appearance, its predominantly brown plumage enabling it to be less conspicuous when nesting. Both birds are strong flyers, much more confident in the air than the red grouse which can sometimes seem to struggle to fly at all.

For everyone who has seen it, the lek is what makes the black grouse so special. Male birds gather together, usually just as the day is dawning, in traditional lek display sites, which are areas of rough pasture, short heather or moorland clearings where there is also good all-round visibility. In some places more than twenty blackcocks will gather, although there are also lek sites where only one or two males turn up to display. The birds crouch and circle the ground, spreading their tails wide, puffing out their throats, inflating their wattles and making a very loud bubbling sound which, on clear days, can be heard over a mile away.

Why a 'lek'? The word may strike southern ears strangely, although Yorkshire speakers will probably find it much more familiar; after all, children in the north of England still *laik* in school playgrounds, the dialect word coming directly from the Scandinavian verb meaning 'to play'.

Although leks take place at most times of the year, they reach their peak in April and May, when the greyhens are also present. Black grouse do not pair for life, so the lek has a key role as the annual talent contest. Females usually lay a single clutch of between six and eleven eggs each year, the chicks becoming fully independent after about two or three months.

Black grouse have declined in numbers for several reasons, one of which has, historically, certainly been the overenthusiasm of shooting parties. Overgrazing by sheep and deer has been a problem, too, as have been changes in farming and forestry practice which have whittled away at black grouse habitats. Black grouse also have predators, especially crows, foxes and stoats.

But, with much effort, things may be improving for the black grouse. Recent surveys in the Yorkshire Dales suggest that the numbers have been increasing, from forty-seven lekking males in 2000 to seventy-eight two years later (the easiest way to get a sense of numbers is to count the number of males displaying at a lek). One important lek site in eastern Arkengarthdale has been monitored particularly closely, and here numbers climbed from eight in 2000 to twenty-three in 2003.

Since 1996, work to assist the black grouse has been co-ordinated in England by the North Pennines Black Grouse Recovery Project, which is funded by, among others, English Nature, the RSPB and the Game Conservancy Trust. The project has undertaken several initiatives, including efforts to improve black grouse habitat. The birds require a range of habitats, such as heather moorlands, upland meadows, rough grazing pastures, open woodlands and scrub land. The birds do not generally venture on to ground above 2000 ft (600 m) or below 650 ft (200 m).

With all these efforts in place to help the species increase in numbers, it can be strange – if not bizarre – to learn that the black grouse remains a game bird which can be shot, perfectly legally, during the season. (The shooting season for black grouse begins a week later than the red grouse season, on August 20, and continues to December 10.) Admittedly, the majority of estates in the Yorkshire Dales now impose a voluntary ban on taking black grouse, but some smaller shooting syndicates may not be quite so scrupulous. The accidental shooting of black grouse during red grouse shoots is also an issue, with the less conspicuous greyhen being particularly at risk. And there seems to be a problem in some parts of the country with shooters bagging blackcocks as trophies during spring lek displays, an act which is clearly against the game laws.

So, paradoxically, one of the results of helping black grouse to become more widespread may be that *shooting* black grouse will also become more widespread. Such is the curious contradiction of the way that game birds are managed and 'harvested'. For the rest of us, however, the sighting of a black grouse remains a highlight of any moorland walk, something to be remembered and treasured.

Black grouse

WALK 11

MALLERSTANG

DIFFICULTY 👟 👟 👟 👟   **DISTANCE 6 miles (9.6 km)**

OUTHGILL   HIGH SEAT   HIGH PIKE HILL   PENDRAGON CASTLE   OUTHGILL

MAP OS Explorer OL19, Howgill Fells and Upper Eden Valley, or Harveys Dales West

STARTING POINT Outhgill (GR 783014)

PUBLIC TRANSPORT A single bus service runs on Tuesdays only, from Kirkby Stephen (station and town).

PARKING There is some informal roadside parking in Outhgill, including a small lay-by beside the church and the verge of the green.

Although short in distance, this walk involves a steep scramble up the side of High Seat and open walking across coarse moorland.

■ The little church of St Mary's in Outhgill was restored in 1663 by Lady Anne Clifford (see page 156)

'after itt had layne ruinous and decayed some 50 or 60 years', as the stone inscription above the porch puts it. A copy of the endowment which Lady Anne made to the church hangs inside, together with other Lady Anne memorabilia.

The churchyard holds the unmarked graves of a number of people who died between

1870 and 1875 during the construction of the Settle–Carlisle railway, which runs a little way up the hillside to the west of Outhgill. Not only navvies died; women and children who were attached to the railway works are also buried in Outhgill, including a mother who died after childbirth together with both her baby twins. A modern stone in the churchyard, erected in 1997, records their memory and their names are given inside the church.

▶ Pick up the lane by Outhgill green.

■ On the green there is a copy of the Jew Stone, a strange stone finger inscribed with Latin and Greek. It was originally erected high on Black Fell Moss, south of High Seat, by a Victorian linguist called William Henry Mounsey.

The story of how Mounsey erected this stone to commemorate his walk along the full length of the River Eden, from the sea to its source on the Mallerstang hillside, is given at the base of the stone, as is the story of how the original was destroyed some years later by railway navvies. The stone was decorated with a Star of David and, although Mounsey was not Jewish, it became known as the Jew Stone. This intrigued Shalom Hermon, a member of the Jewish brigade stationed in Yorkshire during the Second World War, and he was instrumental in arranging for the current replica of the Jew Stone to be made.

For its size, Outhgill has plenty to interest visitors. A little way beyond the Jew Stone, just after the converted barn, is one of a series of 'cone pinfold' sculptures created by Andy Goldsworthy as part of a larger landscape-art project that he undertook in Cumbria between 1996 and 2003.

Andy Goldsworthy has built up an international reputation as an artist who creates sculpture in the landscape using natural materials, such as stone, which are appropriate to the area. The Outhgill cone is one of six which he created in east Cumbria, in what had previously been village pinfolds – in other words, the enclosures where stray sheep or cattle were impounded.

Goldsworthy, who lived in east Cumbria in the early 1980s, says he was strongly influenced in this work by the Nine Standards cairns, the prominent landmarks on the fells north of Mallerstang (Walk 10). He has written, 'I learnt much about the siting of sculpture from the Standards – not least, my own reluctance to place work directly on hilltops. It can be too obvious and at times arrogant.'

He has also described the work of creating the six cone pinfolds: 'I am fascinated by the way a cone grows, stone upon stone, layer by layer – as a tree does, ring upon ring. By making slight changes in the placing of each stone, the shape can be brought out or taken in . . . I enjoy the unpredictability of working by eye and hand. For the most part, my hands are the best tools I have . . .

'Each time I try to achieve a perfect cone but somehow always lose control in the making. Cones dictate their own shape and I resist making "corrections" which might interrupt the flow of form . . . The day I make a perfect cone will possibly be the last time I make one.'

Andy Goldsworthy's cone pinfolds, and the other permanent sculptures from the 'Sheepfolds' project, are the subject of a leaflet published by Cumbria County Council. More information about Andy Goldsworthy's art in Cumbria is also currently available at the Appleby Training and Heritage Centre.

▶ Leave Outhgill behind, and continue on to open ground, initially following a footpath. The footpath peters out as you approach Mallerstang Edge; make your own way across the moor, trying to avoid the wetter ground.

Andy Goldsworthy cone sculpture

To climb the hill safely, aim for the hillside flank between the two prominent valleys of Headley's Gill and Sloe Brae Gill ❶. (Don't attempt to climb the rock scars to the north and south of here.)

It's a stiff climb, but eventually you will breast the hill by a pile of stones.

■ The climb is rewarded by a magnificent view down the valley of Mallerstang, with Wild Boar Fell and Little Fell beyond.

▶ From here, it's a much more gentle climb to the top of High Seat ❷, a short distance away to the east. High Seat is the highest ground on Mallerstang Edge; it also pips Wild Boar Fell on the hillside opposite by just 1 metre (3 ft).

■ For the past twenty years and more, the local rotary club has organized an annual 'Yomp' around the hills of Mallerstang. The full Yomp is a testing 23-mile (37-km) circuit of the valley, which begins and ends in Kirkby Stephen and includes Wild Boar Fell, Swarth Fell Pike, High Seat, High Pike and Nine Standards. The Yomp can be walked or run. The record for fell-running the route is, as the Rotarians put it, 'a barely credible 2 hours 51 minutes'.

▶ High Pike Hill ❸ is almost due north of High Seat. A good track, with regular cairn waymarks, makes the route relatively straightforward in good weather. In poor weather, it may be necessary to rely on a compass bearing.

■ The high plateau between High Seat and High Pike Hill

is remarkable for its landscape of peat haggs, which stand like floating islands above the eroded ground around them.

▶ The descent begins from High Pike Hill. Drop straight off the hillside, aiming west for the

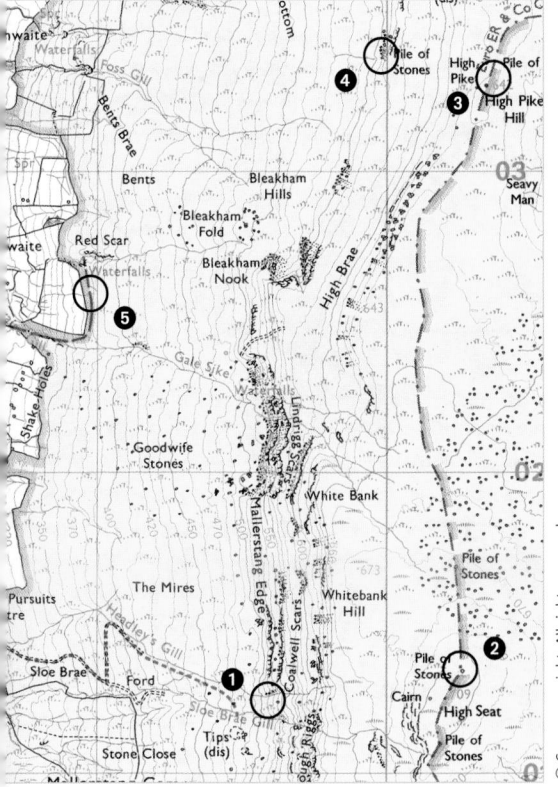

prominent pillar of stones ❹
directly below the hill brow.
This has been well constructed
so that a series of stones extend
out from the main pillar, offering
steps for anyone who might
be tempted to try to climb up
to the top.

The objective now is to cross
the moor, to find the footpath
alongside Gale Sike ❺. To avoid
damp ground, it's advisable
not to lose height too rapidly. To
find the right line off the moor, it
can be useful to continue until
Pendragon Castle appears to be

▶ page 154

Pendragon Castle, in the Eden valley

lined up with the prominent whitewashed farm behind it.

Take the bridleway to the main road and cross to enter the grounds of Pendragon Castle **6**.

■ Pendragon Castle dates back to Norman times and is an impressive ruin in a beautiful location beside the River Eden.

As mentioned on page 156, Pendragon Castle formed part of the estate which Lady Anne Clifford eventually managed to reclaim as her own. She restored the castle in 1660 and it became a convenient stopping point on her journeys between her Cumbrian lands and her castle in Skipton. She notes in her diary that she spent Christmas at Pendragon in the year 1663.

It's perhaps surprising that Pendragon Castle is not more widely known, for it has the benefit not only of a romantic setting but of a name which conjures up tales of Arthurian Britain. According to medieval legends, Uther Pendragon was King Arthur's father. He became King of Britain having returned from exile in Brittany, and later in life fell madly in love with Ygerna, the wife of Gorlois, the Duke of Cornwall. This passion led him to go to war against Gorlois, but Ygerna remained out of reach until Uther Pendragon turned to Merlin for advice.

Merlin, already renowned as a wizard, had a solution. He had, he said, access to some of the latest drugs available, which miraculously would be able to change Uther Pendragon so that the King exactly resembled Gorlois in appearance and behaviour. In this effective disguise, Uther managed to gain access both to Gorlois's castle in Tintagel and to Gorlois's marriage bed. The baby conceived that night was none other than Arthur.

The story of Uther Pendragon's seduction of Ygerna forms part of the legendary history of Britain which was written around 1136 by Geoffrey of Monmouth. His *Historia Regum Britanniae* claimed to tell the story of Britain from its original founding by Brutus, purportedly the great-grandson of Aeneas, to the time of King Arthur and Queen Guinevere. In between, Geoffrey managed to bring in such other mythical figures as the giant Gogmagog, King Coel (the merry old soul and founder of Colchester) and King Leir.

It is by no means clear whether Geoffrey found earlier sources for these tales or whether he simply had a fertile imagination. His material, which he wrote in Latin, formed the basis of much subsequent reworking of the 'history' of Britain by other storytellers, including the poet Layamon, who for the first time told the story in English, and, later, Sir Thomas Malory in his *Morte d'Arthur*.

It would, of course, be helpful at this point to be able to report that Uther Pendragon, according to Geoffrey of Monmouth, resided in a castle beside the River Eden. Unfortunately, Geoffrey says no such thing. The naming of Pendragon Castle could simply have been the whim of its medieval owner – analogous, perhaps, to a decision today to name your bungalow Camelot.

But, of course, that would spoil a good story – and, having seen the delights of Pendragon Castle at first hand, who would really want to do that?

▶ Cross the River Eden behind Pendragon Castle and follow the footpath which runs on the west side of the river to Shoregill. Return to Outhgill.

Lady Anne

Of all the historical figures who have helped shape the story of the Dales, few have left quite such a strong impression behind them as Lady Anne Clifford. She was, by all accounts, a powerful character who acted almost like a queen in the realms she controlled. She knew how to get what she wanted – even if what she wanted was to travel in a horse-drawn coach over some of the wildest moorland country in Yorkshire and Westmorland, where normally only travellers with packhorses chose to go. She was, as one of her aristocratic descendants put it to the editor of the *Dalesman* three hundred years after her death in 1676, 'quite a gel'.

Not everyone was entirely impressed by her strength of character, however. Thomas Gray, best known as the author of the famous 'Elegy Written in a Country Churchyard', visited her grave in Appleby church in the century after her death and commemorated his visit with a parody of an epitaph for her. Gray wrote:

Now clean, now hideous, mellow now, now gruff,
She swept, she hiss'd, she ripened and grew rough,
At Broom, Pendragon, Appleby and Brough.

Gray records the names of four of Lady Anne's domains: Brougham Castle (Broom), Brough Castle, Appleby Castle and Pendragon Castle, all then in Westmorland and now in Cumbria. He could also have mentioned Skipton Castle, at the other end of the Yorkshire Dales, and indeed Barden Tower in Wharfedale. Lady Anne Clifford was a woman with a powerful inheritance.

It was, however, an inheritance which she very nearly didn't receive. She was born, in 1590 in Skipton Castle, into one of the most powerful families in the north. The Cliffords could trace

Lady Anne Clifford

their lineage back to at least the thirteenth century, when an astute marriage had brought them into one of the great baronial families. Thereafter, despite a propensity for regularly getting themselves killed in battle, the Cliffords had done very well, consolidating their estates and, in 1525, acquiring the title of Earl of Cumberland. Lady Anne's father George, who was born in 1558, was the third Earl of Cumberland.

Unfortunately for Lady Anne, however, she was born a girl. Her mother, the Countess of Cumberland, had already given birth to two sons, but both these boys had died in childhood. Keen to ensure that his title continued, George effectively disinherited his daughter, giving his estate on his death in 1605 to his brother, who became the fourth Earl of Cumberland.

The will was complicated and controversial and for much of her adult life Anne would engage in an apparently hopeless struggle to get her estate back. She was helped by the fact that her cousin, the fifth Earl, also had no male heirs – which meant that, legally, her father's property was supposed to revert back to her side of the family. But defending her interests involved standing up to both her uncle and cousin, and indeed to James I himself who weighed in on their behalf.

In the meantime she put up with two marriages to less than perfect husbands, the Earl of Dorset and – after his death

– the Earl of Pembroke. During this time Lady Anne lived in various houses and castles in the south, the places where she was effectively dumped by Dorset and Pembroke. In 1649, however, she finally made the move back north, alone. Two years earlier her cousin the fifth Earl had died and she once again had legal control of her father's old estate. It was in any case a good time to be leaving London: Charles I had been beheaded in January that year, the country was in the midst of a revolution and the capital was probably not the safest place to be.

There was plenty for Lady Anne to do. Her castles and houses were in a poor state of repair and her tenants were disaffected. She stayed briefly at Skipton, visited 'that old decayed tower' at Barden, and then travelled further north to her Westmorland seats. She was at Appleby in January 1650 when she heard of her second husband's death. For the last twenty-six years of her life until her death in 1676 she was to live, probably quite contentedly, as a widow.

One by one, the castles were rebuilt or restored: Appleby and Brougham in 1651–3, Barden Tower in 1657, Skipton in 1657–8, Brough in 1659 and Pendragon in 1660. If Brougham, near Penrith, was perhaps her favourite, she nevertheless travelled regularly between all her castles, staying in each in turn. And this often meant difficult journeys through the heart of the Yorkshire Dales.

Lady Anne, needless to say, undertook these in style. It's perhaps not surprising if her memory is still strong in the Dales, given the impression that her journeys must have made on local people. In *Roads and Trackways of the Yorkshire Dales*, Geoffrey Wright describes her progress like this:

She herself went in a horse-litter; her ladies-in-waiting and gentlewomen were on her coach drawn by six horses; her estate officials and manservants were on horseback, her women servants in another coach, while all the goods and equipment needed by such a retinue were with the large crowd that followed. This of course included the bedding carried from place to place, as well as the chairs, tapestries, curtains and carpets which were also moved from one castle to another to await her arrival.

He adds that the total party must sometimes have been over three hundred strong.

We know the routes that Lady Anne followed from her diaries and other records. Her most ambitious journey was probably the one she first undertook in October 1663 when she made her way north from Skipton Castle, travelling up the Wharfe valley before making the difficult high-level crossing by Stake Pass into Wensleydale. Her route from here was even more challenging. After following the river westwards, probably keeping on the northern slope of the dale, she then tackled the rough track which runs up past Cotter Riggs to Cotter End. There she joined what is now known, appropriately enough, as the High Way, on the moorland edge high up above the valley of Mallerstang.

These were, in Lady Anne's own words, 'those dangerous ways'. The stretch above Cotter End in particular was hardly built for her sort of traffic. As she put in her diary, 'I went over Cotter in my Coach (where I think Coach never went before) and over Hellgill Bridge into Westmorland, so by the Chappell of Mallerstang (I lately repayred) I went into this Pendraggon Castle to lye in it again . . . God pleased to preserve me in that journey.'

It's easy to track down the memorials to Lady Anne's life in the castles and churches she restored. But perhaps the best way to remember this stubborn and determined woman is to walk the High Way above Mallerstang (Walk 12), and to imagine her travelling that way too, dragging her staff and servants through the wild lands on the edge of Yorkshire and Westmorland.

WALK 12

THE HIGH WAY

DIFFICULTY 🥾 🥾 🥾

DISTANCE 11½ miles (18.5 km)

GARSDALE   MOORCOCK   YORE   THWAITE   HIGH   HELL GILL   LUNDS   GARSDALE
STATION   INN   HOUSE   BRIDGE   WAY   BRIDGE   STATION

MAP OS Explorer OL19, Howgill Fells and Upper Eden Valley. Alternatively, Harveys Dales West or Harveys Dales North.

STARTING POINT Garsdale station (GR 789918). Alternatively, the walk can be shortened by starting from the Moorcock Inn (GR 797926); if starting here, on the return leave the suggested route at Lunds church to use footpaths via Blades and Yore House back to the inn.

PUBLIC TRANSPORT Trains on the Leeds–Settle–Carlisle line stop at Garsdale station. There are buses Monday–Saturday from Hawes to both the Moorcock Inn and Garsdale station, connecting with some train services (route 113). Friday buses (route 112) run between Hawes and Sedbergh (with connections from Kendal). A solitary Tuesday bus (route 804) currently runs between Sedbergh and Garsdale and the Moorcock Inn; also on Tuesdays, there is a single bus (route 569) from Kirkby Stephen to the Moorcock Inn. (Check winter timetables for all these routes.)

PARKING Informal roadside parking on the main road near Garsdale station or near the Moorcock Inn

The High Way is well named – an ancient track high up above the Mallerstang valley, with magnificent views. This walk makes use throughout of footpaths and track, though with the option of some open country walking. Be prepared for a stiff climb from Thwaite Bridge.

■ Garsdale is one of the highest stations on the Settle–Carlisle railway, which in turn is the highest main-line rail route in England. Originally called Hawes Junction (this was the place to change for trains down to Hawes and beyond, in the days when there were rails through Wensleydale), the station has a colourful and entertaining history. For instance, the waiting room of the northbound platform was used for a time as a venue for church services, while the ladies' waiting room became a public library of a kind,

after it was given a donation of 150 books. The room at the base of the water tower was used for village functions.

The full story of Garsdale station is told by Sheila Bowker in this book's sister Freedom to Roam guide, *The Three Peaks and the Howgill Fells*. Her book is the place to turn, too, for a walk from Garsdale on to the fells to the west of Mallerstang.

Garsdale station, and the other intermediate stations on the Settle–Carlisle line, are popular today as starting points for walks. However, it was not always this easy to reach the Dales by train. In 1970 British Rail closed the stations on the line to regular passenger trains, leaving just the express trains to thunder past the deserted platforms. In 1974, however, the Ramblers' Association decided that if BR wouldn't take walkers to the Dales, they would: a special excursion train that year was packed with 580 people who came to enjoy guided walks starting from the railway line.

Colin Speakman, a local writer, journalist and active Ramblers' Association member, who was also at that time a member of the Yorkshire Dales National Park Committee, was determined that the Ramblers' charter shouldn't be a one-off. After an initial skirmish with BR, who had originally planned to cut back the station platforms to suit new express rolling stock (a move which would have effectively sabotaged any attempt to bring back stopping trains), Colin wrote to the national park authority proposing that the park itself put on trains for visitors.

'I wrote suggesting the Park should do what the Ramblers had done so profitably, and charter trains to allow people without cars to visit the Dales – and to encourage people with cars to leave them behind and use the train,' he explained. 'I believed then, as I believe now, that this is what national parks were set up to achieve, not as picturesque backgrounds for recreational motoring.'

His idea was by no means universally welcomed, and all kinds of snags and delays had to be overcome. But eventually DalesRail was born, initially as an occasional charter train carrying walkers and visitors into the Dales.

Supporting DalesRail as much as they could were the members of the Friends of DalesRail pressure group, founded in 1980. Guided walks from stations on the Settle–Carlisle line have been the major activity of this group ever since its founding, and the members still arrange a year-round programme of walks (details from www.friendsofdalesrail.org), including regular walks from Garsdale station. The group marked the thirtieth anniversary of the Ramblers' special train with an event in June 2004.

Unfortunately, the start of the DalesRail special trains was not the end of the story. The whole Settle–Carlisle main line was threatened with closure in the 1980s before eventually being reprieved in 1989. The decision to save the line was strongly influenced by the effective lobbying carried out by the Rambler's Association and the Friends of the Settle–Carlisle Line. Today, the line's stopping passenger trains are an integral part of the national rail service.

▶ Walk, with care, along the main road from Garsdale station east to the Moorcock Inn. Turn left on to the road to Kirkby Stephen, and immediately right on to the field footpath which meets up with the lane to Yore House ❶.

Pass directly to the north of the farmhouse and try to find the line of the footpath which runs eastwards a little way above the Ure valley. The path runs just to the south of the Cotterside plantation and, from this point if not before, can be followed relatively easily. It emerges just north of the Ure at Thwaite Bridge ❷.

Turn left at the farmhouse and immediately left again, taking the path which runs up through a little wood. Once out of the wood, the path climbs steeply. Continue into a second field, crossing a track. At the next wall, cross a stile and immediately turn left ❸, to join the old track known as the High Way.

Continue to the hilltop at Cotter End, which is reached near an old lime kiln. From here on it is downhill almost all the way.

■ The High Way is a magnificent track, continuing for several miles on a ledge high above the Mallerstang valley. There are fine views to enjoy, towards Wild Boar Fell and Swarth Fell across the valley and to the southern Howgill Fells.

This is a very old track between Wensleydale and the Eden valley which in its time has seen considerable traffic. In fact, it is because this was a significant historical route, one of the key droving roads of the north-west of England, that the question of whether motor vehicles should be permitted to share it with walkers has become an issue in recent years.

The use by 4x4 vehicles and trail bikes of old green lanes is a controversial subject in the Yorkshire Dales (it is explored in the Freedom to Roam guide *Wharfedale and Nidderdale*). The law is extremely confused on this

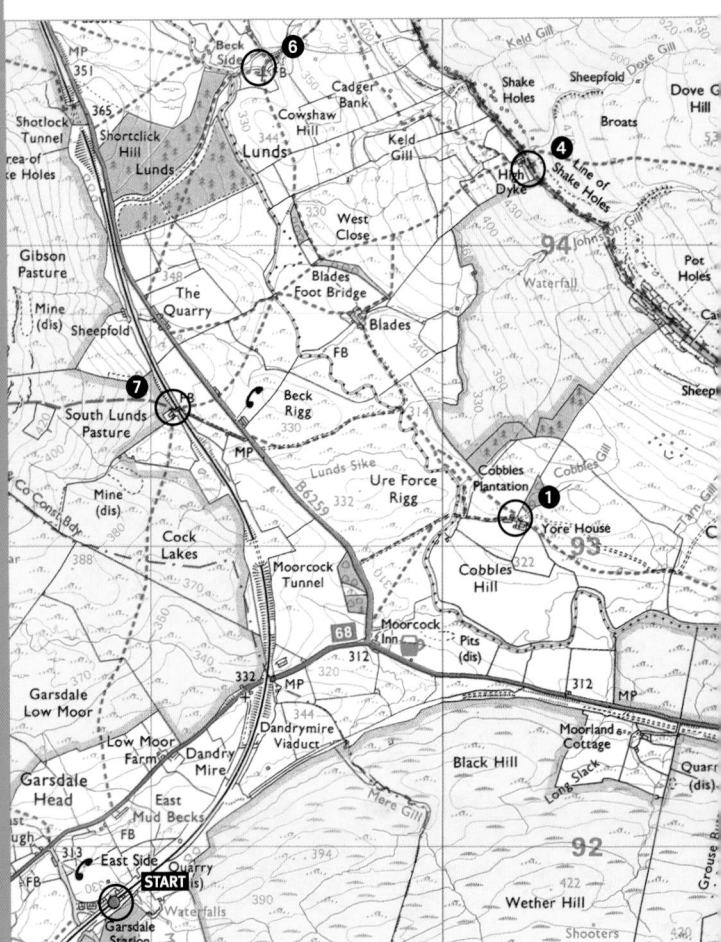

point and several attempts to clarify the legal situation through new legislation have, if anything, only made things more complicated. The government has now said that the fact that a track has been historically used by

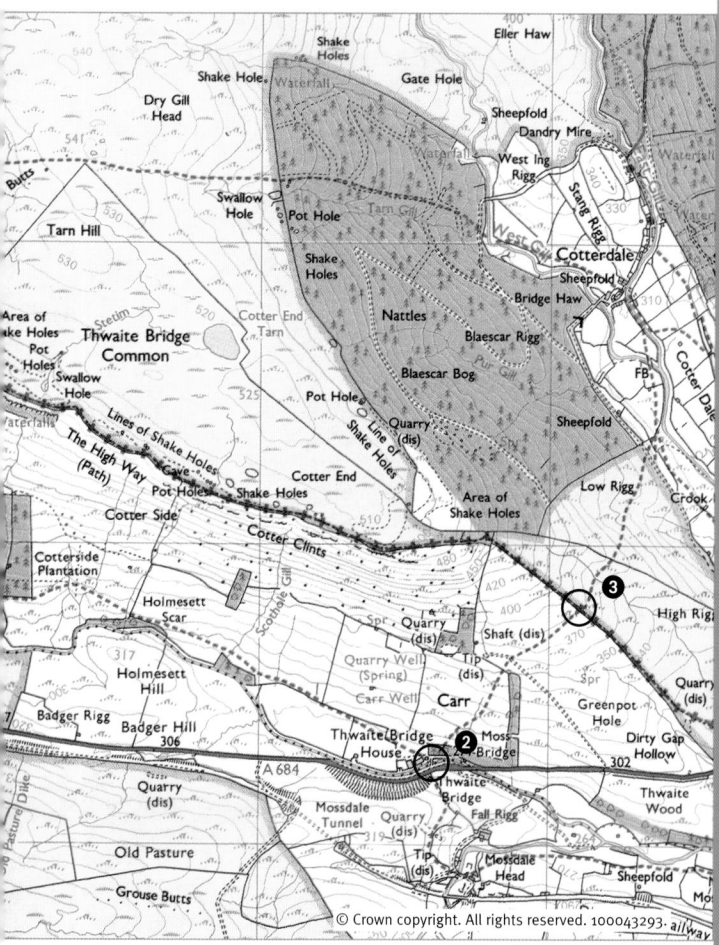

▶ Map continues northwards on page 166

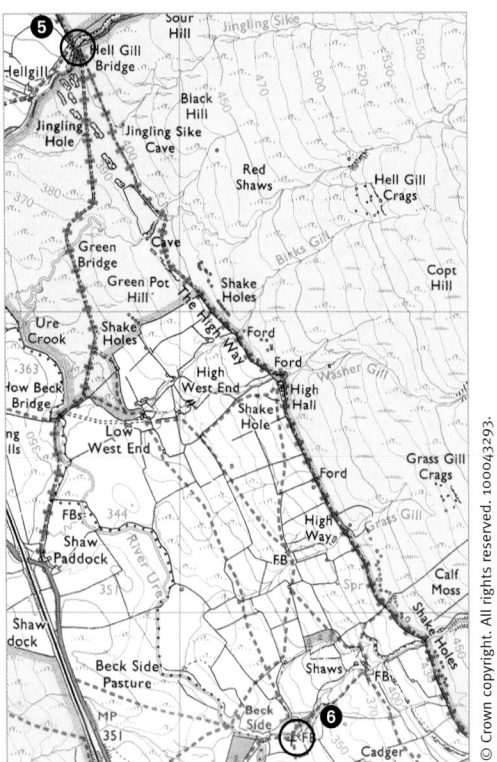

horse-drawn vehicles and carriages should not in itself mean that motor vehicles can use it today, but it will take time before this principle becomes properly enshrined in law.

The Yorkshire Dales Green Lanes Alliance, a local organization set up in 2002, is leading the campaign to keep off-roaders away from the old lanes. They have been helped by temporary vehicle-exclusion orders which have been imposed recently on selected green lanes, including one on a section of the High Way between Cotter End and Hell Gill.

▶ Continue along the High Way for almost 2 miles (3 km) to reach the ruins of High Dike ❹.

■ Unlikely as it may seem today, High Dike was formerly an inn. The existing buildings date back to the seventeenth century, but local historians believe that an inn of some kind probably stood here long before that, offering a place for travellers on the High Way to pause for some welcome refreshment or accommodation.

Drovers would have made up a large part of High Dike's clientele. The tradition of driving animals, especially cattle, over great distances south from Scotland to the markets of England goes back to medieval times, although droving became more widespread in later centuries when political relations between the two countries were more stable. By the time of Elizabeth I the trade had become regulated, with entry to the ranks of drovers controlled through the issuing of licences.

Drovers would be entrusted with the task of leading anything up to a thousand head of cattle over hundreds of miles of country, and with bringing back very significant sums of money from their sale. Drove roads often made for the higher ground, where grazing for the animals was freely available and also, perhaps, where there was less risk of ambush.

The animals would typically travel about 10 to 12 miles (15 to 20 km) a day, and enclosures were needed for them at night. On the moorside by High Way, a little to the north of High Dike near Lambfold Gill, is an old walled field which is thought to have been used as a drovers' enclosure. The field bears the name Horse Paddock.

Drovers were not the only people who came this way. Perhaps the most famous traveller on the High Way was Anne Clifford, the seventeenth-century noblewoman who, as recounted on page 156, chose to negotiate this track by coach, bringing with her much of her household entourage.

Lady Anne left her mark in many parts of the Dales, but the most remote memento of her extraordinary life must be the Lady's Pillar which she erected in 1664 high up on the moors north of here on Hugh Seat. The pillar, restored in the nineteenth century, may have been erected to mark the extent of her landholdings; it may also have been intended to commemorate one of her predecessors as lord of Mallerstang, Sir Hugh de Morville, after whom Hugh Seat takes its name.

▶ Beyond High Dike the High Way continues past another ruin, High Hall, to reach Hell Gill bridge ❺.

While the suggested route for this walk remains on the High Way, those wanting open country have ample opportunity beyond High Dike to head off up the hillside, to explore the flanks of Lunds Fell. The cairns at Ure Head are one possible target.

■ Hell Gill bridge has long been a landmark on the High Way. The need for a bridge here is obvious to all who take a look over the stone parapet: the embryonic River Eden has created an attractive and impressively deep gorge in the limestone directly below.

Hell Gill marks the historic boundary between Yorkshire and Westmorland (now Cumbria). For this reason, the boundary of the Yorkshire Dales National Park was also drawn here when the park was first approved in 1954. This was a somewhat arbitrary decision, which resulted in half the Howgill Fells being included in the park and half being left outside. There are now proposals to revise the national park's northern and western bounds, to include all of Mallerstang and the Howgills.

Mallerstang valley

▶ Turn back from Hell Gill bridge and shortly turn half-right, taking the grassy track which runs down the hillside. The boggy area halfway down is the first trickle of what will very soon become the River Ure – in other words, Wensleydale starts here.

Turn off to reach the farm at Low West End. From here, find the footpath which immediately passes a prominent field barn and then runs on through meadows and rough ground to the farm and church at Lunds ❻.

■ Lunds church was deconsecrated more than twenty years ago, but the old churchyard is a peaceful and evocative place. Bodies were brought here from Cotterdale, along an old 'corpse way' which crossed the High Way near High Dike.

In his 1991 book *High Dale Country*, Bill Mitchell recalls the description of Lunds church given by an earlier writer on the Dales, William Barker, whose *Three Days of Wensleydale* was written for a Victorian audience and published in 1854. Barker reported attending a winter service at Lunds, an experience which obviously lacked something in comfort: the church had lost its door and two inches of snow had settled on the seats and floor. Livestock were kept out of the church by the expedient of wedging a thorn bush in the doorway.

▶ To return to Garsdale, take the footpath south-west from Lunds church to the main road. (The footpath through the wood is difficult to follow and the driveway, although not a right of way, tends to get used by many walkers as a default route here.)

Walk along the main road southwards past the quarry and take the footpath, right, to the footbridge ❼ over the railway. From here follow the well-defined footpath back to Garsdale station.

Some further reading

Here is a selection of books and journals which will tell you more about the area. Please note that not all are currently in print.

C.M.L. Bouch, *The Lady Anne*, self-published, 1954

Mark Bowden and Keith Blood, 'Reassessment of Two Late Prehistoric Sites: Maiden Castle and Greenber Edge', in R. White and P. Wilson (eds), *Archaeology and Historic Landscapes of the Yorkshire Dales*, Yorkshire Archaeological Society, 2004

D.J.H. Clifford (ed.), *The Diaries of Lady Anne Clifford*, Sutton Publishing, 1990

Edmund Cooper, *Muker: The Story of a Yorkshire Parish*, Dalesman, 1948

John Fisher, *The History and Antiquities of Masham and Mashamshire,* 1865

Andrew Fleming, 'Swadal, Swar and Erechwydd? Early Mediaeval Polities in Upper Swaledale', *Landscape History* 16, 1994

Geoffrey of Monmouth, *The History of the Kings of Britain*, Penguin, 1966

David Gerrard, *In the Winds of Heaven: A Portrait of Tan Hill Inn*, CP Printing and Publishing, 1991

Mike Gill, *Swaledale, Its Mines and Smelt Mills*, Landmark Publishing, 2004

Peter Gunn, *The Yorkshire Dales*, Century, 1984

Paul Hannon, *Twenty-Five Walks: The Yorkshire Dales*, HMSO, 1996

Marie Hartley and Joan Ingilby, *Dales Memories*, Dalesman, 1986

Marie Hartley and Joan Ingilby, *The Old Hand-Knitters of the Dales*, 1951; new edition Dalesman, 1991

Marie Hartley and Joan Ingilby, *The Yorkshire Dales*, Dent, 1956

James Herriot, *James Herriot's Yorkshire*, Michael Joseph, 1979

Martin Holmes, *Proud Northern Lady*, Phillimore, 1975

Andrew Hopper, 'The Farnley Wood Plot and the Memory of the Civil Wars in Yorkshire', *Historical Journal* 45, 2002

Frederick Houghton and Hubert Foster, *The Story of the Settle–Carlisle Line,* Norman Arch, 1948

Kenneth Hurlstone Jackson, *The Gododdin*, Edinburgh University Press, 1969

Jack Keighley, *Walks in Dales Country*, Cicerone, 2000

David Leather, *Yorkshire Dales*, Collins, 2003

A.L. Lloyd, *Come all ye Bold Miners: Ballads and Songs of the Coalfields,* Lawrence and Wishart, 1952

W.R. Mitchell, *Fred Taylor, Yorkshire Cheesemaker,* Castleberg, 2000

W.R. Mitchell, *High Dale Country*, Souvenir Press, 1991

W.R. Mitchell, *The Living Moors of Yorkshire*, Castleberg, 2002

Richard Muir, *The Dales of Yorkshire,* Macmillan, 1991

Christopher Partrick, 'Reading Rooms and Literary Institutes of the Yorkshire Dales', in R. White and P. Wilson (eds), *Archaeology and Historic Landscapes of the Yorkshire Dales*, Yorkshire Archaeological Society, 2004

Arthur Raistrick, *The Lead Industry of Wensleydale and Swaledale, Volume 1: The Mines*, Moorland, 1975

Arthur Raistrick and Bernard Jennings, *A History of Lead Mining in the Pennines*, Longmans, 1965

Tom Stephenson, *Forbidden Land*, Ramblers' Association, 1989

Tom Stephenson, *The Pennine Way*, HMSO, 1969

Various, *The Droving Tradition of the Upper Eden Valley* (pamphlet), Eden Arts, 2001

A. Wainwright, *A Coast to Coast Walk,* new edition Frances Lincoln, 2003

A. Wainwright, *On the Pennine Way,* Michael Joseph, 1985

A. Wainwright, *Pennine Way Companion*, new edition Frances Lincoln, 2003

George Walker, *The Costume of Yorkshire*, new edition Caliban, 1978

Geoffrey Wright, *Roads and Trackways of the Yorkshire Dales*, Moorland, 1985

Geoffrey Wright, *The Yorkshire Dales*, David & Charles, 1986

The Countryside Code

An abbreviated version of the Countryside Code, launched in 2004 and supported by a wide range of countryside organizations including the Ramblers' Association, is given below.

Be safe – plan ahead and follow signs

Even when going out locally, it's best to get the latest information about where and when you can go; for example, your rights to enter some areas of open land may be restricted while work is being carried out, for safety reasons or during breeding seasons. Follow advice and local signs, and be prepared for the unexpected.

Leave gates and property as you find them

Please respect the working life of the countryside, as our actions can affect rural livelihoods, the safety and welfare of animals and people, and the heritage that belongs to all of us.

Protect plants and animals, and take your litter home

We have a responsibility to protect the countryside now and for future generations, so make sure you don't harm animals, birds, plants or trees.

Keep dogs under control

The countryside is a great place to exercise dogs, but it's every owner's duty to make sure their dog is not a danger or nuisance to farm animals, wildlife or other people.

Consider other people

Showing consideration and respect for other people makes the countryside a pleasant environment for everyone, whether they are at home, at work or at leisure.

Index

Brough

A66

Bowes

Kirkby Stephen

A685

Richmond

A6018

▲ Nine Standards Rigg

9

B6270

▲ Water Crag
8
▲ Rogan's Seat
8+9
6+8
Keld
6

Outhgill

High Seal

Fremlington

Hipswell

7

Thwaite

Muker

Gunnerside

Grinton

Great Shunner Fell

S w a l e d a l e

B6270

Lovely Seat

Hardraw Force

Askrigg

Whiteside Moor ▲

Castle Bolton

W e n s l e y d a l e

Leyburn

A684

Garsdale Head

Hawes

Bainbridge

Gayle

B6255

Wether Fell

Aysgarth

Addlebrough

B6160

West Witton

Pen Hill

A6108

Dodd Fell ▲

West Scrafton

Great Haw

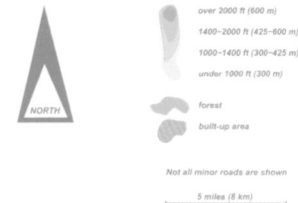

NORTH

over 2000 ft (600 m)

1400–2000 ft (425–600 m)

1000–1400 ft (300–425 m)

under 1000 ft (300 m)

forest

built-up area

Not all minor roads are shown

5 miles (8 km)

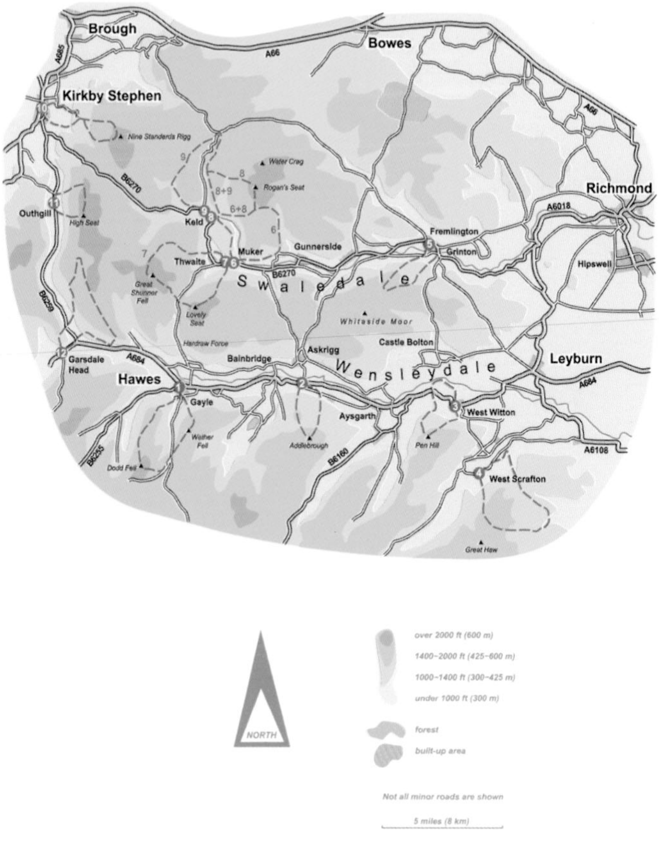